is the first book ever to

ore the phenomenon of

omasochism from both a

ical and practicing point of

v. As the fastest-growing area

exual behavior in the U.S., SM

in recent years received

siderable attention from the

dia – most of it, unfortunately,

e more than cheap titillation,

hout any genuine attempt to

derstand why people voluntari-

participate in sadomasochism.

s is the first book – co-written

JJ Madeson, an SM practitioner,

d Charles Moser, this country's

emost expert in SM behavior–

undertake a serious

amination of the motivations of

ose who choose to participate in

e sadomasochistic lifestyle.

As such, *Bound to Be Free* is a frank and honest examination of a form of human interaction which its practitioners fervently believe is not only reciprocal and loving, but offers them a way of experiencing erotic pleasure deeper than they would get through any "convention- al" activity. The authors study first-person narratives and case histories and finally lay to rest misperceptions and myths surrounding this surprisingly widely practiced form of sexual interaction.

Charles Moser, Ph.D., M.D., is a practic- ing psychotherapist and counselor who has made a long-term study of sadomasochism.

JJ Madeson is an SM practitioner and busi- ness professional. Both authors live in California.

BOUND
TO BE FREE

CHARLES MOSER, Ph.D., M.D.
AND JJ MADESON

BOUND
TO BE FREE

The SM Experience

CONTINUUM ▾ NEW YORK

1996
The Continuum Publishing Company
370 Lexington Avenue
New York, NY 10017

Printed in the United States of America

Library of Congress Cataloging-in-Publication Data

Moser, Charles, Dr.
      Bound to be free : the SM experience / Charles Moser, JJ Madeson.
          p.   cm.
      Includes bibliographical references.
          ISBN 0-8264-0889-3 (alk. paper)
          1. Sadomasochism—Case studies.   2. Sexual deviation—Case
      studies.   3. Sex (Psychology)—Case studies.   I. Madeson, J. J.
      II. Title.
      HQ79.M67   1996
      306.77'5—dc20   95-44572
                                                              CIP

Acknowledgments will be found on page 211,
which constitutes an extension of the copyright page.

To Andy, for opening the door;
To Gabe, for helping me through it;
And to Bobby—always to Bobby—
for making the past, the present and the future
a Wonderful, Exciting, Love-Filled Adventure,
And to the Bay Area SM Community:
I hope we've "done you proud."

And to Michael: I miss you.

JJ

Some . . . may dress in leather; these and others
may play with it. But leather is no affectation;
it is an expression of the soul.

Geoff Mains

Urban Aboriginals

Our sexual energy is literally our life force
at its rawest—no shields, no disguises,
no polite mistaking it for something else.
This is especially true with SM. Sexuality is energy
as tangible as that which turns the earth.

SAMOIS

Coming to Power

Contents

Preface

This book is written to explain and demystify the world of sadomasochism (SM). It is neither political statement nor scientific research. It is, rather, an intelligent, fully informed, fact-based discussion of what SM is, what it means to its practitioners, how it is practiced and the structure of its subculture in contemporary American society.

Serious books about SM in today's culture are rare, and it is no surprise that myths and misinformation abound. With few exceptions, previous works have presented only the viewpoints of outside observers such as psychologists or sociologists: in other words, outsiders looking in. Like all sexual behavior, however, SM is far more than it seems, encompassing an enormous spectrum of physiological and psychological mechanisms. By its reliance only on observed behavior, the outsider's view has consistently led to misconceptions and patently false interpretations of SM behavior.

This book moves beyond the superficial and the inherently misleading, focusing on actual SM behavior by fully integrating the external view of the academic with the internal view of the SM practitioner. JJ Madeson has been an active participant in the SM subculture for fifteen years, and a frequent lecturer on the subject before academic and nonacademic groups; Dr. Charles Moser is a physician, sexologist, licensed clinical social worker, and respected academic researcher specializing in the study of sadomasochism. By collaborating, we have attempted to provide a point of view that is uniquely accurate, sensitive, and fair in its depiction and interpretation of erotic sadomasochism.

In candor and fairness to the reader, we state our belief that human sexuality is positive, and that a very wide spectrum of sexual tastes and desires is normal: Sex is okay. SM is okay. Despite the rampant myths and lurid press that surround sadomasochism, nothing in our collective research, clinical practice or personal experience has convinced us that there is anything inherently wrong, immoral or unhealthy about this mode of sexual expression.

While we will briefly discuss the history behind the perception of SM as an illness or a "deviation," our view is that SM represents nothing more than one choice from the vast menu of sexual possibilities. It is, for the overwhelming majority of its practitioners, a loving sexual option. Done responsibly, it is as safe and as pleasurable as any other sexual activity. There are "breast men" and "leg men"; there are women who are turned on by men's buttocks, their hands or their eyes. Likewise, there are people who are turned on by SM. It is that simple.

Our purpose is to guide the reader toward a clearer understanding of the realities of sadomasochism, because we believe there are natural curiosities about the topic, because fear of SM is unnecessary and because the only way to alleviate such fear is through education.

To understand our subject matter, you will need to suspend your preconceptions about SM—or be willing, at least, to question them. Even if you have seen SM behavior in movies, or read about it in books or magazines, be aware that these portrayals are often misleading; the physical activities taking place are only part of the experience. As important are the psychological and emotional components of SM sexuality that cannot be fully or accurately depicted on film or in literature, and virtually none has even attempted to do so. Rather, we ask the reader to look through the eyes of knowledgeable observers and participants to see the deeper love and tenderness inherent in SM play—because SM *is* about love, sex, tenderness, trust and respect.

> Everything within an SM exchange is done with the intent of producing physical or emotional pleasure.[1]

We do not speak officially for the SM community, but we believe that the majority of that community will agree with the observations and perceptions we present here. In fact, the experiences and emotions described in the following pages are gathered from those in the SM community—acquaintances, clients, friends and lovers. While we have altered some details and deleted all names to preserve their privacy, the substance of their comments and views has not been changed.

Part I of this book (Chapters 1–3) is the work of Dr. Charles Moser, based on his extensive research and clinical experience—plus the invaluable insight provided by JJ Madeson as an SM participant. In Part I, the term *we* refers to both the authors.

Part II (Chapters 4–12) was authored by JJ Madeson and expresses the views and experiences in her fifteen-year odyssey of discovery, expression and acceptance of her own erotic SM sexuality. As co-author, Dr. Moser provided critical perspective and a scientist's discipline to the work in this section. Part II thus represents JJ's intensely personal account, and the word "we" in the balance of this book refers to herself and to the members of the SM community who have supported and contributed to her effort.

Throughout this book, indented text indicates that an outside source has been quoted. Quotes from published scholarly literature are attributed to the author in the text, and a full reference to the published work is provided at the end of the book. We have also provided extensive quotes from private writings and newsletters published by and for the SM community which are also fully attributed in the endnotes. When the quoted material is excerpted from interviews and conversations with SM practitioners, however, we have not identified the source by name, gender or primary sexual orientation. As you will discover, men and women, heterosexuals, homosexuals and bisexuals, singles and couples, young and old, experience heartfelt feelings in relation to their dominant or submissive roles and the sadomasochistic lifestyle.

We need to add one caveat before we begin: Although it is by no means our goal to proselytize, there may be some readers who find a personal attraction to the SM world or to some of the activities discussed. Please be careful: SM can be dangerous or abusive in the hands of novices or pathological personalities. We would urge you to contact an SM group in your area, or you may get in touch with us care of our publisher.

We hope that by the time you, the reader, close this book, you will be far more knowledgeable about the real world of erotic SM. Whether or not you approve, you will have gained insight and expanded your horizons. In this, we commend you for your courage.

LOVE LETTERS

The following letters are reprinted with the permission of *DungeonMaster* magazine, a gay SM publication. These letters appeared in the January 1985 issue.

The letters are from a submissive in bondage and the dominant who placed him there. We reprint them here in full because they are expressively loving and because they articulate so clearly some of the deep emotions at work in the Sexual Magic of SM.

Here I am inside, bound, helpless, vulnerable. The man who bound me can keep me here for as long as it pleases him. He can display me to others or just leave me alone.

There is time now to dwell upon my condition, consider my limits, concentrate my will and stamina to stay the course. I want to prove myself to myself as well as to [him].

I MUST endure this bondage. I am forced to live with it—in it. I abandon myself to a fate totally beyond my control. And the deeper the restraint infuses my spirit, the more it liberates, and—yes, gives freedom!

And all the time there is a stirring warmth, a sense of unutterable joy in my loins, and [even] orgasm, though eventually desirable, is now unimportant. The whole trip is an orgasm. I occasionally drift away from the consciousness of my surroundings; my senses do turn off from time to time, and I'm left with only the struggle of my mind to come to terms with isolation and discomfort; to transcend, and be released from pain by the sheer force of my will.

I'm proud to be here. It turns me on to know that the person suffering, struggling, exhilarated and satisfied—is me. *The more I'm bound, the freer I feel.* I'm glad to have others know this.

Bondage means different things to different people. To some, it's the means to an end; to others, an end in itself. It's as awesomely beautiful to behold as it is to experience. It's aesthetic as well as erotic; mental as well as physical.

True bondage is inescapable bondage; it is when my Top puts me into restraints from which I cannot free myself. The man who binds me, binds me to himself as the instigator and perpetrator of whatever agony and ecstasy is to follow.

I start by indulging in fantasy, then grow inward, and finally retreat from superficial reality into true reality.

If we understand each other, if we have a rapport, he may then take me deeper, and as I approach my endurance limit, he will help me to steel myself against the Panic. The ultimate, and the most rewarding, aspect of bondage is that moment when I feel that I cannot endure another second of the restraint, and I cry out for release. But he, my Top, is there to guide me through the barriers of my limits.

I would not want to fail him, much less myself. He knows that I always try *not* to use a release code—that despite my pleas and whimperings, his is the judgment, his the decision. Then my "Thank

You" for the trip from Heaven to Hell and back is heartfelt and sincere.

Thank You, Sir.

There you are, inside the little cocoon that I have made for you. I have put you there, and for my purposes and enjoyment, you shall stay. You have given up all rights: the right to see, the right to hear, the right to move about as you please, the right to sensation and feeling. You have not thrown them cautiously to the wind but have placed them firmly in my hands, knowing full well that they will be returned to you.

You may think it took a long time to put you in this position; in truth, it took years.

Sometimes it truly blows me away how much of yourself you give to me in this moment, and how much responsibility that involves when I accept it from you. The trust that you imply, simply by being in the position that you find yourself, is overwhelming.

Do you realize, little one, that in my own sadistic way, I can take away your right to breathe?

Why do I do this to you? What do I get out of it? I am an artist; I have used you to create something of great aesthetic beauty. I am an exhibitionist; I get off on the sighs and whispers from [any] onlookers; the admiration of fellow Tops; the desire of other bottoms.

I am a sadist. I enjoy the look of you, the knowledge that with each passing moment, you are in torment, and I need not lift a finger. I am also your biggest fan. I silently root for you, supporting you in going the distance I have set, cheering you on, and proud of you when you win.

Thank YOU!

PART 1

Through the Looking Glass

Come, journey with us into the world of sadomasochism, a world of sexual variation, excitement and love, joy and freedom, limited only by the vast boundaries of the imagination.

Introduction: *Dr. Moser*

I have always been fascinated with sex, academically and personally, and was lucky to find several professors in college who encouraged me academically. When I found an advertisement in an underground newspaper for an SM meeting, I was interested and curious enough to want to go, but with the stereotypes about SM still firmly entrenched, I was petrified.

Once there, I was so scared that I literally did not say a word during the entire evening. While some of the people tried talking to me, I could do nothing more than shake or nod my head!

At one point, our small group of newcomers were asked to form a circle, and introductions began with an attractive young woman who said, "My name is Tracy and I'm into heavy pain, heavy humiliation, and I belong to John." The next woman, a pretty blonde, said, "My name is Gilda; I'm into heavy pain, heavy humiliation, and I belong to John." The next speaker was a short, middle-aged, bald black man who said, with a big smile: "I'm John."

The next person introduced herself as a nursing student doing a term paper on SM, but added, "I think I may be interested in this personally." She then exhaled her cigarette smoke directly at John, who was staring determinedly at her. As soon as the meeting was over, John and the student nurse made a beeline for each other.

I was fascinated by the whole thing, went to several more meetings and began asking questions. This laid the groundwork for my later graduate studies. I researched the small amount of traditional literature available on the subject, but I found that the SM people I was meeting did not fit these stereotypes.

My decision to do this book was in answer to the questions people were asking me about SM: "Why do people do SM? What's wrong with them? What is SM really about?" Since none of the current books on the subject answered these questions adequately or addressed the issues to my satisfaction, I decided to write one.

At about the same time, JJ mentioned to me her desire to document her SM lifestyle and the impact it had had on her life, so we joined forces. With her personal experiences, knowledge and insight into the SM lifestyle and my experience as an interested and trained observer, we shared the same goal: to educate and help others to understand what SM is and what it is not. I believe it is important for us to understand SM behavior in order to comprehend more generic and socially approved human sexual behaviors.

SM is probably the least understood and the most feared sexual behavior. We seek here to expose the myths and lessen the fear for, as you will discover, SM is a safe sexual game; it is role-playing in the sexual arena, and what is thought of as weird, kinky, and a rare phenomenon actually is not. These individuals dare to be involved in an activity that breaks some of our most deeply held social taboos. They face extreme prejudice; thus they must keep their activities secret. They are afraid of what their employers, family or friends would do if they were to be exposed as sadomasochists. These fears are well-founded: SM participants have lost jobs, family and friends if their interest in SM is discovered. While most of us would be ashamed to be accused of being a racist, a sexist or homophobic, bias against SM practitioners does not elicit the same outrage. My hope is to add to the knowledge base and let people make informed decisions. My own view of the scientific data suggests that SM is just another valid sexual variation and is not pathological. I hope to convince you of this by the end of this book.

1

Definition

There is a paucity of research on the subject of sadomasochism in our society, the people who practice it and what common characteristics, if any, they share. Research has failed even to agree on a clear definition of SM.

The narrow picture of what is sexually acceptable doesn't describe the great range of human sexual expression.[1]

▼　▼　▼

Here is a list of things SM is not: abusive, rape, beatings, violence, cruelty, power-over, force, coercion, non-consensual, unimportant, a choice made lightly, growth blocking, boring.

Now a list of things SM is: passionate, erotic, growthful, consensual, sometimes fearful, exorcism, reclamation, joyful, intense, boundary-breaking, trust building, loving, unbelievably great sex, often hilariously funny, creative, spiritual, integrating, a development of inner power as strength.[2]

▼　▼　▼

The relation of love to pain is one of the most difficult problems, and yet one of the most fundamental, in the whole range of sexual psychology. Why is it that love inflicts, and even seeks to inflict, pain? Why is it that love suffers pain, and even seeks to suffer it? In answering these questions, it seems to me, we have to take an apparently circuitous route, sometimes beyond the ostensible limits of sex altogether; but if we can succeed in answering it, we shall have come very near one of the great mysteries of love. At the same time, we shall have made clear the normal basis on which rests the extreme aberrations of love.[3]

Since physician Havelock Ellis wrote the paragraph immediately above, none of the questions he posed have been adequately answered, and ignorance about sadomasochism, even among academic sexologists, is rampant.

In fact, the Marquis de Sade (actually the Comte de Sade) was born in 1740 of a noble and ancient French family. He was an early sexologist; his writings were a catalogue of everything sexual, especially sexual violence. The characters in his writings were rarely consenting; thus he was not really writing about what we now call SM. Interestingly, SM practitioners rarely find de Sade's writings erotic today. He was incarcerated for most of his adult life and had virtually no opportunity to experience the things he wrote about. His writing style came to be called "le sadisme," and psychiatrist Richard von Krafft-Ebing coined the term "sadism" from this writing style rather than from de Sade himself.

Leopold von Sacher-Masoch was born in 1836 in Austria, one hundred years after de Sade, and appears to have been what we would now call a masochist. His father (Sacher) was a police chief; his mother, the daughter of an eminent public-health physician (Masoch). Dr. Masoch was known to have convinced the Austrian government to put sewers in Vienna, preventing epidemics and raising the general health of all Vienna. When Dr. Masoch's daughter married, the Prince allowed the hyphenated name and use of the knightly "von" as an honor to the family.

Based on Sacher-Masoch's novels—the most familiar of which is the classic *Venus in Furs*, an insightful and partially autobiographical account of a man's complete submission to a woman—Krafft-Ebing correctly understood these novels to depict Sacher-Masoch's concept of sexuality, and thus used the family name of the author as descriptive of this new category of psychiatric diagnosis. Leopold was understandably upset at this use of his family name and wrote a letter to Krafft-Ebing expressing his outrage. Nevertheless, Krafft-Ebing persisted and named his new form of sexual psychopathy after a public health physician who probably never engaged in any masochistic acts, but whose grandson was a gentleman novelist who extolled the virtues of pain and suffering.

While these are the objective historical facts, a practicing sadomasochist views it somewhat differently:

Both de Sade and von Sacher-Masoch were fearless in their erotic fantasies. De Sade was a bitter and scandalous social critic; he can easily be misread. Together they showed us their understanding that our fiercest fantasies come from the same place as our tenderest loves. They deserve honor, not blame, for opening this truth to us. Krafft-Ebing was wrong to take their names for sickness; moralists and too-ardent feminists are wrong to take their names for evil. And we sadomasochists are right to reclaim those names, to take them back again for something which, for us, is a good and positive experience.

Finally, in 1895, psychologist Albert von Schrenk-Notzing linked the terms *sadism* and *masochism* into "algolagnia," a reference to the connection between sexual excitement and pain, and in 1938, Sigmund Freud first combined the two terms into one: sadomasochism.

Gilles Deleuze, a professor of philosophy at the University of Paris, did a comparative analysis of de Sade and Sacher-Masoch in his book *Masochism*, concluding that

> The two men lived in such different worlds (in time and space as well as mentally) that the linking of their names in the term "sado-masochist" is truly ironic. Yet, there they are, married for all time, immortal (some would say "immoral") and inseparable."[4]

To continue this discussion, we need to explain a "cultural paradox" with which we have lived for over a century and to which we have all been exposed:

> Descriptions of these sexual behaviors are so compelling that the media can always bank on their depictions to stir the interest and increase profits. At the same time, we condemn these behaviors, which we do not understand, and regard people who make [this] a regular part of their lives as intrinsically different, frightening [and] wrong.[5]

Although somewhat simplistic, the source quoted above defines sadomasochism as "the deliberate use of physical and/or psychological 'pain' to produce sexual arousal."

> SM's actions direct the mind away from the outside world and create a heightened awareness of the body, its limits and its instincts.[6]

On the other hand, the public's concept of SM, exemplified by a *Time* magazine article in 1981 concluded: "While that kind of behavior

... may be rare, it is a sobering reminder that SM is no sport, but a driven activity fueled by rage."

We begin now to perceive the source of much misunderstanding. Unfortunately, the English language makes no distinction between "the criminal sadist who enjoys causing desperate agony [and even death] in a victim and the sexual sadist who seeks . . . fulfillment with an eager and consenting partner."[7]

> At the risk of ruining our well-tarnished image, we must tell you that the picture of the evil sadist abusing the cringing masochist is not quite the reality. In fact, no sadist we know would pull the wings off a fly unless the fly said that it would enhance its sexual pleasure.[8]

Often, even those who participate in SM-type behaviors are hesitant to use the term "SM" because sadomasochism is such a loaded word.

> SM is a loosely defined subculture. Much SM is gentle, and many of the gentler practitioners prefer to call this "DS" for Dominance/ Submission. They use "SM" for the pain and rough stuff!
>
> ▼ ▼ ▼
>
> The [SM] experience is an exaggeration of the usual sexual encounter, and its excitement derives in part from its uniqueness.[9]

Let us be clear and unambiguous, therefore: This book is *only* about the consensual form of erotic SM which is widespread in modern society. All references to sadomasochists (or SM) by the authors and by SM participants refer to this mutually consensual and mutually pleasurable eroticism.

The terms "sadomasochism" and "SM" are used interchangeably throughout this book, but a slight distinction does exist. "Sadomasochism" is the term used by the scientific and professional communities while "SM" is the term commonly used by participants to define their activities and is used here without pejorative connotations. The relationship between these two terms is analogous to the distinction between the terms "homosexual" and "gay."

Outsiders, however, apply the term "SM" to a wide variety of distinct behaviors. Those who practice erotic SM as part of their lovemaking and lifestyle require much more narrow and specific terms in order to identify compatible partners and negotiate a "menu" of lovemaking activities. These more precise descriptors are extremely useful in understanding the emotional and sexual components of SM behaviors.

"Dominance and submission" (DS) describes the deliberate transfer of psychological and sexual control from one partner to the other, implying scenarios of sexual submission and servitude which may be erotic in themselves (with or without elements of bondage, physical pain or humiliation).

The term "Bondage and Discipline" refers to sexual scenarios in which various types of physical restraint are used to heighten the intensity of the experience (bondage), while Discipline refers to the acting out of fantasy scenarios that contain a punishment/reward theme such as "teacher/student" or "drill sergeant/young recruit."

> Bondage serves to restrict movement so that the submissive's energy is more where I want it to be. It works as a form of sensory deprivation. If you're tied up, your entire attention is only on what you feel; you can't go anywhere else. It works as a focus.
>
> ▼　▼　▼
>
> Some people struggle in bondage but I see no point in wasting that energy. I relax into it, and it makes me very helpless, which is scary. But if it's done by a top who's sensitive, it's also very erotic.
>
> ▼　▼　▼
>
> I like delicate bondage a lot. I think it's very beautiful; I love the aesthetics of it. I like the visual bizarreness of hoods and masks and fetish clothing. It turns me on.

"Humiliation" refers to role-playing scenes in which the dominant partner has been granted the power to subject the submissive partner to ritualized and carefully circumscribed psychological torment—typically, requiring them to perform openly submissive acts or to participate in forms of sex which may be, to the general public, perceived as "degrading." These scenarios often include verbal insult, usually confined to sexual issues.

"Sadist" and "masochist" also have different and more specific meanings when used *by* sadomasochists. These terms identify those people who experience erotic pleasure by giving or receiving carefully controlled sensations of pain—most commonly in the form of spanking or whipping. These experiences are primarily physiological in nature, although they are always sexual in content and may also be overlaid with psychological roles of domination and submission.

Among homosexual men, the term "leather" is used broadly to indicate those gay men who enjoy SM and to describe sadomasochism itself—as in "a leather bar" or "the leather scene." The same term is used by and about SM-identified lesbians.

Other, far less prevalent behaviors are also generally categorized within sadomasochism, including infantile role-playing by adults, "forced" feminine dress of submissive males and eroticized scenarios involving urination or excrement.

While we are exploring the SM lexicon, it is interesting to note that terminology works both ways. The SM community has coined the term "vanilla" to refer to sexual intercourse and other more conventional forms of lovemaking without any SM component. The word "straight" is also applied to non-SM sexuality.

With so many behaviors existing as distinct erotic preferences, so many possible combinations being distilled within unique, personal scenarios, and so many words to describe them, it is no wonder that scientists have failed to produce a precise definition of sadomasochism.

Even SM practitioners themselves disagree on how to define their own SM behavior. Nonetheless, their subjective explanations of their feelings and experiences are probably as close as we will come to understanding.

Thus, we must look to the players themselves for definitions of what they do, and each participant in the world of sadomasochism has deep feelings as to what they believe it to be:

> *Defining* SM is easy: It is erotic psychodrama based on deliberate roles of domination and submission. We act out, fulfill and make real our erotic fantasies. But *explaining* SM is hard. It is multileveled art, full of paradox, and seldom what it seems.

▾   ▾   ▾

> Uninformed and inexperienced minds had dubbed these sexual traditions sadism and masochism, but giving and receiving pain are only the facade. SM is a mystical union, enrapturing the dominant in a rush of power and dissolving the will of the submissive, granting her, in its place, the freedom to experience pure sensation.[10]

▾   ▾   ▾

> SM is a thoughtful and controlled expression of adult sexuality that holds the promise of intense intimacy and sharing.

▾   ▾   ▾

> Few can deny that it's the most intense sexual experience they've ever encountered. For us, the intensity ranks first, hands down.[11]

▼ ▼ ▼

SM to me is an exchange: first and foremost of trust, and then of respect. I think true SM is a level of consciousness, a "mindspace" that the players get into: a feeling of euphoria, of power and, ultimately, of gratification. And knowing, no matter which end of the whip you're on, that the two of you have created this electric connection, this magic. That, to me, is the ultimate beauty of SM.

▼ ▼ ▼

My idea is that SM is all-encompassing. It's "sex," but that term seems so limited. It's emotional; it's spiritual; it's physical. It just has to do with everything! It's being very, very close to someone and hiding nothing.

▼ ▼ ▼

I think SM is a sexual alternative. It's positive, consensual, loving. I'm not talking about violence or brutality. I'm talking about two people wanting to be there, wanting to have the experience, knowing what the experience is, and trusting that the other person will take them to a good place. It's like a drug, and you can get high on its energy.

▼ ▼ ▼

It's a lot of things. There's the SM—the physical intensity. Then you have dominance and submission, in which there need be no pain, in which the dominant controls the submissive by mental or physical means, but who really does take control. Or you can have both. Either way, the focus is trust, because in SM done with love, there has to be trust on both sides.

▼ ▼ ▼

SM is an exploration of the frontiers of the human experience conducted alone or in small groups. It employs pain/pleasure, catharsis, coordinated forms of physical and mental stress, and sensual, indulgent experience to yield, on occasion, transcendence. These are intensely euphoric, even ecstatic experiences.

As we see in the statements above, love is most definitely a part of the SM Experience. Indeed, Havelock Ellis broke with tradition and not only rejected the popular idea that SM was based on cruelty, but was the first "outsider" who dared to suggest that much of this behavior is motivated by love:

When we understand that it is pain only, and not cruelty, that is the essential in this group of manifestations, we begin to come nearer to their explanation. The masochist desires to experience pain, but he generally desires that it should be inflicted in love; the sadist desires to inflict pain, but he desires that it should be felt as love.[12]

And from the inside:

How can we possibly equate SM with love? Aren't the two at opposite poles? Not at all! In a one-to-one relationship, each person gives to and receives from the other by expressing themselves, at the same time, still catering to the partner's needs. No rational, intelligent human being could or would devote as much time, energy, and creativity as SM demands to a partner he dislikes or for whom he has no feelings, just as no sensitive lover could achieve true sexual pleasure unless he knows that his partner likewise achieves full satisfaction. It necessarily follows that SM is, and must be, an expression of love.

Ellis also understood that masochists limit their love of pain to sexual situations, and that the sadist is concerned with the sexual pleasure of the "victim" as well as his or her own, and we support this belief:

Sure, there are people, I guess, who like to be victims. Women, men, everybody. SM is different. As a submissive, I take responsibility for and accept the part of me that wants to be a victim by deliberately *playing* the victim. I put myself in a safe situation with someone I care about where I can get that part of me acknowledged. So I don't have to go out and get the shit kicked out of me and have people take advantage of me all the time; I can handle those parts of me better this way. And it's much more fun.

▾ ▾ ▾

When I'm dominant, I'm loving him because he is loving me for hurting him. And I love that!

▾ ▾ ▾

We power-trip people all the time. Human beings enjoy controlling other people. We don't have politicians and war and power games for nothing. It's inherent in what human beings are. Our society says that, on the one hand, we should be aggressive and strong, but on the other hand, don't be a bully. There are mixed messages here.

▾ ▾ ▾

So instead of denying the dark side of yourself, denying that sometimes you'd really like to hurt someone, denying that you sometimes like to be hurt, in SM you accept it. And you accept it in a context where there are other people who really enjoy that side of you and that it's a conscious, safe space in which you can express that part of yourself. In SM, there's a beginning, a middle and an end; it's a game, it's sexual and it's fun. But it is both an expression of love and of that dark side that we all have.

▾ ▾ ▾

We're bombarded by choices and decisions every day. It's a much more complicated world than it was. So to relax, to be able to give up for a while, not have to make choices and not have to make decisions—to accept, rather than be on guard and in charge—it's truly exhilarating. To be in a situation where thoughts are wiped out for a while, where you have breathing space for just a time, that's SM.

In 1969, Paul Gebhard, director of the Kinsey Institute, published "Fetishism and Sadomasochism." This was an important contribution to the study of SM since it laid the foundations for SM's examination as a social behavior rather than as a manifestation of individual psycho-pathology. It was not until the late 1970s, however, that serious and objective scientific research on sadomasochism began.

In 1977, Andreas Spengler published the results of his study on a sample of West German male sadomasochists he had contacted through membership lists of SM clubs and organizations. His subjects were not psychiatric patients, and his focus was on the social aspects of sadomasochism.

Over time, attempts to study and define SM have become less judg-mental and more realistic by recognition and acceptance of the premise that SM is a consensual activity whose goal is pleasure for all participants.

Sadomasochists obviously agree:

Outsiders and beginners often see SM as bizarre and destructive. Some think that sadists do whatever they want to masochists and that masochists somehow enjoy suffering. But real-life masochists are *choosy* about their ordeals, and sadists always have to think about the masochist's post-party affections— the relationship when the restraints come off. So behind our appearances, our fantasies and the games we play, SM is something that we sadists and masochists do together . . . for fun.

▾ ▾ ▾

I don't see this particular kind of sexual activity as "kinky" or strange. Instead, it is one of the many ways open to me to share energy, creativity, and love with others. Through SM, I am able to express the wonderful and seemingly opposite aspects of my nature. I have the freedom to behave submissively or dominantly, to acknowledge my masculinity and my femininity, and to take emotional risks. I love the empathy that exists between us when we explore the very nature of pleasure and pain. As a bottom, I love the feeling of being helpless yet the object of affection and desire; as a Top, I love the feeling of being in control while carefully gauging and meeting the needs of my partner.

▼   ▼   ▼

This form of making love allows me to experience complete trust and to joyfully acknowledge all of my sexual and emotional needs. To me, the beauty of SM is in its paradoxes: Through the intensity of pain, we give ourselves more completely to each other than in perhaps any other way; through the exploration of fantasy, we are more honestly ourselves than at perhaps any other time.

▼   ▼   ▼

When it's right, my God, it's like . . . I squirm and moan and everything feels so good. It's an ecstasy that you can't put into words. You can't paint it; you can't photograph it. You can only feel it. It's in your mind. It's just there and you can't know the freedom of it until you experience it.

In a significant 1984 study, Williams, Weinberg, and Moser[13] found that SM behavior usually contains five components: the appearance of dominance and submission, role-playing, consensuality, sexual context, and mutual definitions. Specifically:

1. *The Appearance of Dominance and Submission:* Dominance is the *appearance* of rule over one partner by another. The dominant partner is variously called sadist, dominant, dominatrix, top, master, or mistress. The counterpart to dominance is submission, the *appearance* of obedience to a partner. The submissive partner is variously called masochist, submissive, bottom, or slave.

It's play-acting but it seems real because there are two different personalities in me: The little girl in there that needs to be spanked and humiliated is not the same woman who wants to see men crawl at her feet and get them really hard and turned on and tease them and make them do what she wants. They're both me, but they're different aspects of me. I believe that if people tap into the different parts of themselves and play with them in the erotic context of SM with someone they trust, their lives get richer.

So I get to be that little girl who needs a certain kind of input and punishment but who really doesn't fit in my life as a grown woman. And there's a space, too, for my desire to overpower men. It's a whole lot better than screaming at the clerk at the store because he gave me the wrong change. You find a place for expressing different sides of yourself and things balance out.

▼   ▼   ▼

As you grow older, you start putting limits on yourself, and society starts putting limits on you. It's only the child who can break through those limits and do what he or she wants. Children can play. I don't believe that adults get to play— unless they're acting like children— or doing SM! It's so neatly laid out really, so simple. SM is a "game" with "toys"; we pick our roles and we "play"—just for fun, no other reason.

2. *Role-Playing:* An *exaggeration* of those sets of expectations that surround the interaction between the dominant and submissive roles chosen, such as master/slave or teacher/student.

As a Top, I've gotten drunk on the bottom's energy. It's a delicious place to be, that place where I am hurting somebody who wants me to hurt them. And yet I know when to stop and realize that it takes two to do this. I'm a loving sadist working together with a loving masochist.

3. *Consensuality:* A *voluntary* agreement to enter into dominant/ submissive "play" and to honor certain "limits." We cannot call spouse abuse SM because SM is consensual and spouse abuse is not. Just as the difference between intercourse and rape is consent, so the distinction between SM and true violence is also consent.

If there is one constraint that is almost universally applicable throughout the leather community, it is that the acceptability of an action must be agreed upon by both the partners. One's limits must be recognized and any transgression must be a willing one. There are strong social sanctions reserved for individuals who break this trust. Indispensable to this understanding of limits is an appreciation of oneself and of the multifaceted attributes of the human self.[14]

4. *Sexual Context:* The presumption that the activities have a sexual meaning. SM is primarily a sexual behavior; while it need not mean orgasms or erections, it is nevertheless sexual. We are not denigrating

such behavior in nonsexual contexts (e.g., religiously motivated flagellation); we are just clear that this is a different phenomenon.

　　5. *Mutual Definition.* The participants must agree on the parameters of what they are doing, whether they call it SM or not.

In summary, then, SM is erotic, consensual, and recreational. It is heavily dependent upon fantasy and the illusion of control, and requires collaboration and mutual definition in order to be satisfying to the participants. While the range of SM activities is quite varied, we find that when participants categorize their activities as SM, all five factors are usually present.

　　Sadomasochistic activities themselves can involve a continuum of physical sensations (or lack of sensation, as in sensory deprivation play) ranging from the gentleness of a kiss to intense pain produced by, among other things, spanking, slapping, whipping, caning, piercing, etc. SM play often involves the use of specialized paraphernalia (known as "toys") such as whips, riding crops, shackles, clamps, handcuffs, dildoes, rope and blindfolds (to mention just a few!), fetish objects such as leather clothing and, almost always, the enactment of erotic fantasies.

　　While we will explore the issue of sexual pain in greater detail later, for now we point out the common myth that all SM involves pain. In fact, SM does not always involve physical pain. Even when pain is present in an SM scene, the reader should bear in mind here that the interpretation (definition) of pain is culturally bound. Also, what appears to be painful to an observer may not be painful to the recipient. The hickey (or love-bite) is the best example of this phenomenon. It would be painful to be bitten suddenly on the neck, but in the passion of a sexual interaction, a hickey is often felt as pleasurable.

　　The focus of SM is most often the interaction between the players, the dominant and the submissive, and this is, in fact, its primary appeal for most SM partners. For others, it is what the pain *symbolizes* (i.e., that one is completely in control of, or under the control of, another person) that is erotic. It is not our intention to deny the importance of pain to many sadomasochists, but it is important to understand that definitions of SM that focus exclusively on pain miss the essence of the SM Experience: the ritualization of dominance and submission. Therefore, a sexual interaction without pain can still be SM, and pain in a sexual context is not always SM.

So, finally, for purposes of this book, we will adopt the following definition of SM:

> *Consensual, erotic interactive behaviors played out by partners deliberately assuming, for one, the dominant role, and for the other, the submissive role, where the role-playing forms the context for the activities, and where the behaviors can, but need not, include the use of physical and/or psychological pain to produce sexual arousal and satisfaction.*

What Do We Know
about Sadomasochism?

SM behaviors are seen throughout history, dating back at least to ancient Egypt and to the Hindu culture in India where books like the *Kama Sutra* portrayed sexuality as an art form wherein the "erotic arts were not only deemed worthy of respect but were thought to be divinely revealed."[1]

Western religion has always taught a receptivity toward certain elements often present in SM: suffering is frequently praised as a purifying force in Biblical literature and is graphically portrayed in Catholic sculpture and paintings of the martyred saints. The dominant/submissive dynamic is explicitly described and praised in a variety of relationships: God/man, King/subjects and husband/wife. Paradoxically, the mainstream religions of the West also profess a specific aversion to dominant/submissive sexual expression. Indeed, the puritan philosophy, a form of religious expression historically part of the American culture, "does not consider any action meritorious," says Theodore Reik in his 1941 book, *Masochism in Modern Man*, "if it is not connected with discomfort [and deprivation]."[2] This same philosophical bent can be found at the heart of many religious beliefs including those of Catholicism and Judaism, and some of the societal taboos surrounding SM can be traced to such religious beliefs.

Ford & Beach found that even preliterate cultures employed "painful stimulation techniques" as acceptable additions to one's sexual repertoire and alluded to others. Interestingly, they also conclude:

[Often] societies in which intercourse is regularly associated with biting, scratching or hair pulling prove inevitably to be ones in which children and adolescents are allowed a great deal of sexual freedom. . . . Furthermore, if the cultural stereotype of satisfactory intercourse includes a considerable amount of moderately painful interaction, that stereotype also represents the woman as an active, vigorous participant in all things sexual— she is accorded equal rights of initiative and is expected to experience orgasm as a result of coitus.[3]

SM-type behavior is known even in the animal world where Ford & Beach contend that biting and aggressive behavior are common. Kinsey et al. (1953) noted twenty-four different mammals that bite during coitus, and Gebhard (1976) concluded that "from a phylogenetic viewpoint, it is no surprise to find sadomasochism in human beings."

In the late fifteenth century, the first unambiguous case of SM was reported by Pico della Mirandola, who described a man who enjoyed sex only if beaten bloody with a whip dipped in vinegar. In 1516, Coelius Rhodiginus discussed a man who found a severe whipping to be a sexual stimulant, and Otto Brundel in 1534 reported the case of a man unable to have intercourse unless he was whipped. These cases, however, were seen as medical curiosities and not as psychosexual illnesses (Ellis, 1903/1936).

Although exploring only the history of masochistic references, Roy F. Baumeister states that he finds no record of such activity before 1500 and no historical record until the seventeenth century.

Then, abruptly, in the 18th and 19th centuries, there is abundant evidence of sexual masochism. Thus, sexual masochism is a modern phenomenon. Moreover, masochism is quite unusual in this respect: Most of the modern sexual practices, including many that would be considered deviant today, were familiar to the ancients.[4]

During the late 1800s and the early 1900s, sexologists began exploring all sexual behavior. Many of the European sexologists were Jewish, enabling Hitler to label sexology a "Jew Science," eventually crushing the early sexological movement by imprisoning or killing these researchers throughout Europe, and burning their papers and books. Thus, much early understanding in the area of sexuality— including SM—was lost.

While Havelock Ellis saw sadism and masochism as two complimentary emotional states, Sigmund Freud in 1938 introduced the combined term *sadomasochism* and noted that such states could be found in the same person. Additionally, Freud called this previously unremarkable behavior a "perversion," defining sadism as "an aggressive component of the sexual instinct" and masochism as "a continuation of sadism directed at one's own person," further helping to establish sadomasochism as a clinical entity.

As a result of Krafft-Ebing's influence, the categories of sadism and masochism became available as diagnoses of sexual pathologies (disease). The pathological connotations are still evident; both sadism and masochism are defined as paraphilias (aberrant sexual activity) and listed as "mental illnesses" in the American Psychiatric Association's *Diagnostic and Statistical Manual (DSM) of Mental Disorders.*

In their review of sexual attitudes throughout history, Bullough & Bullough conclude, "Sadomasochism is a good example of the way a pathological condition is established by the medical community, for until it became a diagnosis, it received little attention and was not even classified as a sin."[5] Moreover, the sadomasochist was only one of a number of sexual categories that were invented beginning in the nineteenth century; others were "pedophile," "transsexual," "fetishist," and "homosexual."[6] To recognize the historical roots of this classification is to understand that the "sadomasochist" is a socially constructed category.

> What they do may seem extreme, but it is done with honesty and care, and it is couched in affection.[7]

Such categories perform certain functions. To the public, it makes sense of what appears to be bizarre behavior. Indeed, the term "sadomasochism" is extensively used (especially by the media) to refer to a variety of behaviors that involve sex and violence, e.g., lust murders, rape, and spousal abuse. It is also employed in cases where sex is not involved at all, e.g., referring to a strict drill instructor as a sadist or the wife who stays with an alcoholic husband as a masochist. For professionals, the term reflects the increasing "medicalization of deviance"—that is, defining the behavior as a medical problem or illness.

> The things that seem beautiful, inspiring, and life-affirming to me seem ugly, hateful, and ludicrous to most other people. This may be the most painful part of being a sadomasochist; this experience of radical difference, separation at the root of perception. Our culture insists on sexual uniformity and does not acknowledge any neutral differences—only crimes, sins, diseases, and mistakes.

Most of the psychological literature is bent on demonstrating that alternate (which I prefer to "deviant") sexual practices or lifestyles are in some way sick. This is a consequence of the medicalization of psychology. I'm not very happy that psychology is seen as a medical process. It seems to be far more a philosophical issue.[8]

▾   ▾   ▾

In our context, outsiders perceive sadomasochists as weird and kinky simply because we seem to enjoy activities most people consider negative, painful, undesirable, degrading.

When asked, however, how I justify these things, my answer is: I make no attempt to justify them. They are activities I choose to perform within the privacy of my own home or some other private setting. I do these things with willing adults, and I am not particularly concerned with how the rest of society regards me.[9]

▾   ▾   ▾

My behavior does not involve anyone but me and my partners. It certainly doesn't involve "the rest of society"; why not just leave me alone?

Many previous studies and books about SM have been almost exclusively based on case studies of those in therapy specifically seeking to overcome SM desires, so it is no surprise that many researchers and therapists have concluded that such people are "sick." It should be noted, however, that there is no scientific study that indicates SM practitioners in general suffer from any specific psychological problems or that their choice of sexual behaviors in any way interferes with their day-to-day functioning. What has been established is that there are now, and have always been, people engaging in SM behaviors who are happy and functional members of society.

And yet as a whole, the leather community presents a profile of stability and security. They appear to have found forms of self-adaptation that puts life within a meaningful perspective.[10]

The concept of SM as a deliberately chosen sexual preference is relatively new, and there are few studies that address the incidence of SM behavior in our society.

There were nineteen scientific surveys on human sexual behavior published before Kinsey's famous volume, *Sexual Behavior in the Human Male* (1948) and of those, only one dealt with any aspect of SM at all. Kinsey collected more than 18,000 sex histories from all over the United States via an interview format. The minimal data concerning SM behaviors were reported in the second volume (1953), where Kinsey found that twenty percent of the men interviewed and twelve percent of the women had at least some erotic response to sadomasochistic stories.

Considering the negative attitudes towards SM, it is extremely difficult to find willing participants in SM research, and the reticence of participants to admit their interest is understandable. Differences in definition of sadomasochism also make estimating difficult. Current estimates of the number of people who practice sadomasochism range all the way from five to fifty percent of the population.

Today, television, music videos, records, movies, and books, both fiction and nonfiction, portray SM more explicitly than ever before. The most recent examples of such creative attention to SM includes films (Blue Velvet, 9½ Weeks, Body of Evidence, Basic Instinct) and books (9½ Weeks [McNeill], Exit to Eden [Anne Rampling], the Beauty Trilogy [A.N. Roquelaure], Men in Love [Nancy Friday], Erotic Power [Gini Scott], Different Loving by Gloria and William Brame and Jon Jacobs [1993] and the highly publicized 1992 Sex, by Madonna). A delightful book called Screw the Roses, Send Me the Thorns is the newest entrant into the world of SM literature. Its authors, Philip Miller and Molly Devon, discuss many of the whys, wherefores and how-to's of SM with a wonderfully humorous sense of play.

"Western society," says the late Geoff Mains, author of Urban Aboriginals, "would rather not face a good deal of what confronts us but like many before us, the sadomasochistic community refuses to be completely silenced."

Like most modern countercultures, sadomasochism exists on the margins of western society where one finds the surviving shards of older sects like witchcraft. To these same shores are attracted explorers on paths such as shamanism, oriental religion and the occult. It is on these cultural fringes that the SM Experience has long found a relative acceptance. Significantly, on these same fringes are often found many of the thinkers, artists, and eventually shakers of western culture.

3

~~~

The SM Individual
Who Are Those Guys Anyway?

There is a misconception about the people involved in the Scene [the SM community]—what we term "Ted Bundy-itis." When you discuss S&M, the first thing people think about is a Ted Bundy type, preying on unsuspecting women and getting sexual kicks by maiming and killing. It's as far away from the Scene as it is from mainstream society.

The people in the Scene are, by and large, older, more intelligent, and probably better off economically than the average person. These are contributing and respected members of society: our next-door neighbors, our parents, our brothers and sisters, our teachers, and our doctors, Hollywood's brightest stars and the grocery store's nicest cashiers, our politicians and our clergy.[1]

An insider answers the question "Who are we?" this way:

We are people of all ages, all races, all religions, all political views and both sexes. We can be found in every area of the earth at every socioeconomic level and in just about every occupation. We are tall and short, thin and fat, attractive and homely, intelligent and not-so.

But despite these differences, we share many experiences in common in terms of our sexual desires: We all believed at first that these desires were ours alone, that they existed only in our imaginations. We found we couldn't shake these thoughts, and we knew that they did not conform to "acceptable" social behavior. We could tell no one . . . until we found each other. We often feel unforgivably different simply because the drummer we follow is our own.

Research does indeed support these words. SMers represent all races, creeds, religions, socioeconomic classes, and sexual orientations. While it is often reported that sadomasochists tend to be above average in both education and affluence, we acknowledge a potential bias here in that it is probably the better educated and more affluent individual who is most likely willing to participate in the research studies on which we base these beliefs. It is also important to note that research subjects are most often members of organized SM groups or advertisers in SM contact magazines; it is obviously more difficult to find those individuals who are more private about their sexual practices.

While the SM community welcomes anyone with a sincere interest, those participating in the organized subculture are most often in their middle thirties or older. People in their twenties, for example, as with almost any alternative lifestyle, tend to be "just trying it on for size"; often, their presence in the SM community is both tentative and short-lived. As we shall see later on, the strength of character and level of maturity needed to cope with SM as a lifestyle is often lacking in these younger "explorers." Sometimes, these young people will pop into the Scene and then pop right back out, finding little in common with the older, more sophisticated participants other than their sexual interests. They often come back into the Scene as they grow older and more mature, for the desire to live such a lifestyle can be irresistible.

The available literature supports few general statements about those who participate in SM activities. In fact, no study has demonstrated that SMers possess any special psychological characteristics that set them apart in any way from the general population.

By way of example, in *Masochism: A Jungian View*, published in 1982, analyst Lin Cowan writes that her clients are

> ... successful by social standards: professionally, sexually, emotion-
> ally, culturally, in marriage or out. They are frequently individuals
> of admirable inner strength of character, possessed of strong "coping
> egos" and with an ethical sense of individual responsibility.

In her 1983 book *Erotic Power*, sociologist/anthropologist Gini Scott concludes:

> A vast variety of people with a diverse range of erotic interests partici-
> pate in [SM]. . . . Their backgrounds, activities and attitudes are quite
> unlike the social stereotype that depicts [SM] as a form of violence,
> mischief, or mayhem perpetrated by the psychologically unstable
> who seek to hurt others or to be hurt themselves. . . . At the core of the

... community are mostly sensible, rational, respectable, otherwise quite ordinary people. Thus, quite unlike its public image, the community is a warm, close and supportive one.

In *Masochism & the Self* (1989), Roy Baumeister, a professor of psychology at Case Western Reserve University of Cleveland, Ohio, pointed out that

> ... most live normal, well-adjusted lives. Apart from their sex lives, they are pretty much like anyone else. [It] is not a sign of being sick or maladjusted. In the modern era of individual rights and sexual tolerance, it seems ridiculous to condemn an otherwise normal person for a basically harmless sexual preference.
>
> The appeal of [sado]masochism is in its effects on the mind. [It] is a powerful means of escape from everyday life, from problems and worries, from who [we] are most of the time.

Research studies to date neither support nor negate a developmental cause for SM behavior. This means that research has been unable to pinpoint any early behavioral clues that would indicate a specific individual may become a sadomasochist. While research will undoubtedly continue in this area, judging by the vast diversity of individuals involved in SM, it seems unlikely that such behavioral clues will be found.

In discussing childhood sexual memories and fantasies with sadomasochists, we find that most such remembered experiences tend more to indicate a degree of dominance or submission within the young personality than a desire for SM itself. The need for research on this issue is tempting: Of those who eventually adopt SM as a "sexstyle," do the SM roles (dominant or submissive) in which they feel most comfortable correlate in any way with whatever developmental dominant or submissive behaviors were exhibited in their early years? Did they, in fact, exhibit dominant or submissive behavior in their childhood years? Were their youthful dreams and fantasies indicative in any way of the sexual role they came to adopt as adults?

So are sadomasochists mentally ill or psychologically impaired? Is SM "sick"?

> Not so long ago, psychiatrists would have considered these people to be mentally disturbed for even having, let alone exhibiting, their deviant erotic tastes. But over the past few years, students of human behavior have discovered that the safe, consensual practices of sadomasochism, dominance, submission, bondage, discipline, and other

forms of erotic power exchange are not as rare as they once were thought to be. Moreover ... the individuals who engage in such practices are usually normal, healthy folks, much more likely to be your lawyer, auto mechanic, school teacher or grocer than one of the mutant aliens portrayed in B-movies and pulp fiction.[2]

For mental health professionals, one of the most informative gauges used in determining the seriousness of mental illness, from simple anxiety to psychosis, is the patient's ability to function realistically in the day-to-day world. Contrary to the view held by much of the psychotherapeutic community, there are no data supporting the view that the psychological functioning of self-identified sadomasochists is impaired in any way.

Needless to say, sadomasochists themselves hold strong views on this issue:

There is a tendency to describe anything that violates the norms of the times as "sick." It is not a scientific concept but a moral one hiding behind the mask of pseudo-science. A body may be sick or well as defined by biology because a properly functioning body is an objectively determinable phenomenon. Proper behavior, however, cannot be prescribed by science. It is a philosophical matter, one involving value judgments which cannot be arrived at by the scientific method.[3]

▼ ▼ ▼

It needs to be seriously asked: Can the capacity to experience pleasure ever be called a sickness? The capacity to experience pleasure is a precious gift; it should be treasured and cultivated, not treated or cured.

▼ ▼ ▼

I think SM lets us explore our full potential, both in personal pleasure and in social growth. Repressing "deviant" behavior will solve nothing. Let us try to understand it rather than judge it. Let us try to see the positive values that are to be found in it if we only look for them.

▼ ▼ ▼

The positive value of SM has never been properly understood outside our own circles, except more recently by a fringe of people who have taken the time to find out what the practices are all about. Of course, the fear of SM will probably always be there, because the repressed SM component within people's basic personalities is so nearly universal. Recently ... some students of social science [have] recognized SM practices as an enormous catharsis, the healthy venting of energies that might otherwise prove destructive.[4]

Psychoanalytic theories that attempt to explain the development of sadomasochistic desires in an individual are quite different from sociological explanations whereby these people develop a concept of self as a sexual being, realize these needs, find other people with whom to act them out, and, finally, begin to establish an SM identity. While psychoanalytic theories and the many generalities found therein do not appear relevant to the identity development of SM practitioners, these same generalities do form the basis for many of the stereotypes about sadomasochists.

Examples: sadomasochists were abused children; they were sexually aroused at an early age by family or academic corporal punishment; they were raised by alcoholic, violent, or unstable parents, and their own personalities tend toward violence.

Quite to the contrary, there are no data from objective studies to support these theories or the belief that as adults, SMers are abused or abusive spouses. Those people who, in their rage, abuse others deny their victims the key element that separates SM from violence: Consensuality. We will discuss this issue in greater detail in chapter 5.

In addition, as Moser's 1979 study found,[5] less than twenty percent of the sadomasochists studied could recall ever receiving erotic enjoyment from childhood punishment. We are candid to say, however, that we do know a few SMers who were abused as children, but whether their past experiences have in any way influenced them towards an interest in SM is not known.

While few doubt that large numbers of men participate in sadomasochism (usually assumed, incorrectly, to be gay), little is known about the women involved in the SM world. In 1977, Andreas Spengler indicated that a few female prostitutes were associated with some of the West German SM clubs he studied, and concluded that "if one desires to go beyond individual case studies or studies of sadomasochistic prostitution, it is almost impossible to question sadomasochistically-oriented women in the subculture; there are hardly any nonprostitute ads and very few women in the clubs."[6]

Soon thereafter, however, Dr. Moser's 1979 survey, along with a few similar studies, have shown that there are, indeed, many female sadomasochists, both lesbian and heterosexual. Indeed, Dr. Moser's study was one of the few to identify and include a sample of women, but he is candid about the sample's shortcomings. The perception that few women participate in the SM subculture reflects the difficulty in obtaining a sample, because women have been much less likely than men to join sexually oriented groups or advertise for partners in SM publications. Today, computer bulletin boards and other technological communication media attract as many women as men. Further, the reality is that there are large heterosexual and lesbian SM communities worldwide.

A question often asked of those who study sadomasochism regards the number of people who actually practice it. To our frustration, we must once again say we simply do not know. We can, however, make an educated guess. Using as our gauge the results of studies of sexual behavior as well as sales of SM paraphernalia, books, and magazines (including pornography), the mail order SM business, classified ads seeking SM partners and the demand for SM professionals, we believe that about ten percent of the general population are actively involved in SM with some recognition that their interests are specifically sadomasochistic; another twenty to forty percent may engage in SM behaviors without knowing their activities could be so defined.

Almost everyone knows people who are into SM. Because of the stigma, they may not be willing to tell you about it, but you know them. There is a good chance, then, that out of every ten men or women you know, one will be interested in SM.

~~ PART II

Beyond the
Looking Glass

Join us now on an in-depth tour of the SM subculture, a unique look inside a world that few outsiders ever see, guided by sadomasochists themselves, for who better, after all, to act as our guides? It is a hidden world, a secret and intimate place where those society does not understand find solace, companionship and the opportunity to explore sexual fantasies in a safe, non-threatening atmosphere.

> We're living out our fantasies. We have that opportunity; we've taken that risk. I believe most people would really like to do some of these things. I think many people fantasize about it, but for a variety of reasons, they never get around to trying it. We, on the other hand, take our dreams and fantasies and live them! That's what we're really doing, and we're having a wonderful time doing it!

As we begin this section, we would remind the reader that the word "we" in the balance of this book and "I" in text refers specifically to JJ Madeson and the San Francisco Bay Area SM community of which she is a part.

Introduction: *JJ's Story—Welcome to My World*

I lie naked on the bed, arms and legs stretched wide, ankles and wrists tied firmly to the bedposts. Blindfolded, I am acutely aware only of sound and physical sensation. Intense, unique feelings. The whip whistles through the air and falls—gently at first, then harder— on my breasts, stomach, legs, genitals. I struggle to squirm away from the blows, but it is futile. I am helpless to move even a little away from the sting of the whip. My body is covered in sweat, my throat is dry . . . but there is a lake of excitement between my legs.

As the whipping continues, harder and harder, the pain becomes intense beyond reckoning. My senses are overloading; I feel dizzy, as if I were floating. Finally, one deep sigh . . . and there is quiet calm. I am aware only of the sound of his breathing, my own, the noise and shock when the leather strands hit, for they have not stopped. On some level, I know that what is happening should hurt—should hurt a lot, like it had moments before—but I feel no pain; I have forgotten that it hurts.

It is as if my body has given up all tensions, all cares; as if I were free of the world for that time, floating gently in space in a state much like meditation. There are often tears at this point, for the sense of release and peace is overwhelming. Were there some other experience that would give me the same exhilaration, I might be doing that instead. But only SM has given me this freedom.

Why do I love SM? I have no better answer to the "why" of SM than to the "why" of any other variable of sexual attraction. Why do women get turned on by men's sexy eyes; why are pretty legs attractive to some men and big breasts attractive to others? Why do I get turned on by pain? I don't know.

I once believed that if I sought and experienced sexual pain, if my sex partners hurt my body, I would be less vulnerable and better protected from emotional pain; if they could hurt me physically, they couldn't hurt me emotionally. It also occurred to me that if I could feel the pain, I knew I was "there." It was a plea, a way of saying, "Hurt me if you will but don't ignore me," an idea articulated most clearly by Leo Buscaglia, lecturer on love and happiness, when he stated, "If I had to choose between pain and nothing, I'd choose pain."

My theories, of course, were unprovable but were sad commentaries on my youthful sense of self and the loneliness that served as a justification for the kind of sexual desires I had. With maturity and understanding, I have grown away from these speculative theories. My sense of self is secure and I am no longer lonely. I have found my home.

And so . . . I do love SM. And I do like sexual pain, which is probably the hardest part of the SM Experience to explain. There are those involved in SM who do not like pain, who are not "into" pain. But this is my story, and as part of my involvement in SM, I *am* into pain. I don't know why; I just am. Among other things, it is often specifically the intensity of the pain that creates that final push into the peace, freedom, and calm I seek. I admit it—I am an intensity junkie.

But there is more to me than a love of sexual pain, and there is more to my passion for SM than simply the pain. The following pages should give you some insight into who I am, both as a woman and as a sexual being, as well as the reasons behind this book. Do not look for specific answers, though, to the "why" of SM, for it is found deep within, almost too deep to articulate. Rather, look to the reason, the goal: An intense experience in which is found freedom, excitement, love, peace— and FUN. Maybe that really is the Why.

When I first began writing this section, it contained many pages of autobiography and included my ideas on sex education, masturbation, etc. My co-author read it. "Very interesting," he said, "but something's missing. Try again." We discussed it for a while, and as we talked, he asked me what SM meant to me.

"It's obvious," I said. "SM changed my life. It's the hottest, scariest, most intimate, most exciting thing I've ever experienced."

"That," he said, "is what *JJ's Story* should say."

So here I am, back to basics. Welcome to my world.

The fact is that sadomasochism did change my life. Never have I experienced anything so psychologically potent, so physically powerful, so emotionally satisfying. Never have I felt as free, and the freedom is longer-lasting than just the duration of my SM play. It is a continuing freedom and courage to explore myself, the people and the world around me from a position of inner strength that, before SM, was lacking in my life. Since SM has come into my life, I have been freed to be the glorious, loving woman I always knew was in there.

The road has not been easy, but for me and many thousands of those similarly inclined, it has been worth it. Even now, after fifteen years, it is difficult to put such strong, emotionally charged feelings into written words, so if the thoughts expressed here seem unusually emotional, forgive the dramatics—my feelings run very deep.

Early in my SM life, after I had come to accept the SM part of me, I attended a party at the Catacombs, a gay men's "playhouse" used occasionally for heterosexual SM group parties. It was a sinister looking place, filled with black leather slings (like hammocks), chains, motorcycles bolted to the floor (really!), and an atmosphere that screamed out: "INTENSE!"

I arrived at the party with a date and a woman friend who, entering the place for the first time, was immediately intimidated. On the other hand, I instantly felt a sense of "Oh, yes, I've come home!" It was a strong and sure feeling. That was the first time, but by no means the last, that I felt so centered, so okay around my chosen lifestyle; the first time I was so sure about myself as a part of this world.

Sadomasochism is not an easy lifestyle choice; indeed, it is fraught with dangers and scary things. It is, all at the same time, frightening, erotic, awkward, exciting, and socially unacceptable. I have lost a job and friends because of my lifestyle. These are high prices to pay for a sexual experience, but I believe I have no choice. Once I discovered SM, tried it, liked it, adopted it as my own, it became an undeniable part of me. The risks and costs exacted by society can indeed be extreme; it would be easier to conform. But for me to deny SM would be like denying I am a woman. It is that clear.

What can I tell you about myself that will explain all of this, that will help you to understand?

My upbringing was average; my sexual interests normal. I grew up in a middle-class home with one sister and parents who were openly loving. I was never abused, physically or in any other way; I was never a victim. I was, however, a difficult child: bright, rebellious, emotional.

Unfortunately, no one in my family knows ANYTHING of this lifestyle I have chosen, and this saddens me. But I love them too much to hurt them, and I believe this knowledge would hurt them because they would not understand. They know I am happy, and that is their main concern. But I cannot share with them the greatest source of my happiness. I sincerely wish it could be otherwise.

My sex life until age thirty-five was active but "according to the norm," the standards set for women growing up in the fifties and sixties. I enjoyed sex but there was rarely any variety or exploration of new things. The "missionary" position without orgasm was standard for me, and even oral sex was a little "kinky!" No one ever came along to suggest that it could be otherwise.

I remember masturbating infrequently—there seemed little need or purpose. At some point, though, around age twenty-five, I remember developing (or renewing forgotten memories of) a masturbatory fantasy that involved doctors, medical instruments, examinations and a great deal of humiliation. The orgasms this produced were earth-shaking, but it took days to get over the guilt and embarrassment of having such fantasies, and the guilt was not worth the earthquake it momentarily created in my body. I also thought I was the only person on earth with this kind of fantasy (a common misconception). The key elements in this fantasy were the presence of a "do-er" (for me as a confirmed heterosexual, this was always a man) who would do things to me, always against my will; I was the passive one and, for the first time, played the sexual fantasy "victim."

At about the same time, I realized that I liked "rough sex," the idea of sexual struggle. That was the only way I could describe it: just the exhilarating rush of pleasure when a man, in the heat of passion, ran his fingernails down my back . . . hard. The next day, the scratches were a tingling reminder of the pleasure of the night before. I didn't always want gentle (although I always wanted affection and tenderness), but it was difficult to find a man who understood this. I was never much good at explaining it, for these thoughts had no name, no label, no category into which they fit. Then—as now—I do not claim to understand why this turned me on. It just did. And obviously it still does; it's been more than fifteen years!

After trying conventional marriage, I found myself alone in 1980 in San Francisco, the "anything-goes" capital of the country. As I sat in my apartment one evening, KQED, a public television station, aired an explicit documentary called: "SM: One Foot Out of the Closet." I was fascinated. I was virtually unaware that SM existed, and what I saw that night scared me to death . . . because it tugged at me; it turned me on. These were, in some way, MY fantasies that were being played out. There was the gentle and the rough, the tender and the hard. The activities discussed and demonstrated by *real* sadomasochists seemed almost familiar—much more intense than I was willing at the time to deal with, but my God, people "out there" really DID these things! There were even organized groups! I may have felt like a freak and a pervert in my desires, but I now knew, at least, that I was not alone. It was like living in a cave for a lifetime, never knowing that sunlight existed. The sunlight was blinding. I was stunned, but unprepared to act, so the show rattled around in my mind for a while.

A few months later, the station aired the show again. This time I was ready. Pen and paper in hand, I watched, noting options, terminology. I was intrigued but fearful, for I knew even then that the taboos against sadomasochism were strong, and I felt myself being pulled in some very scary directions.

One of the organized groups mentioned on the show that appealed to me the most was for heterosexual male dominants and female submissives. At the beginning, submission just seemed the most comfortable choice for me—it still is— and was in no way a denial of my own personal strength. Indeed, the majority of SM beginners—men and women—come in as submissives. It is easier simply because the skill and knowledge necessary to be a dominant require more experience. In general, even among the more experienced of us, there are more "bottoms" (submissives) than "Tops" (dominants).

But finally, I had to face the truth. There WAS something here that interested me. I was terrified, and yet I wanted to try it—whatever "it" was. But there was no one I knew or could trust to support me in my search. Where to begin?

Getting bolder, I called the *Spectator* (formerly the *Berkeley Barb)*, a local sexually oriented underground paper, figuring that someone there might direct me to this group. The man who answered the phone was hesitant, questioning my reasons for wanting contact with the group. I explained that "I—uh—might be—uh— interested in the things they do." There, it was out. Then he called my bluff: He said that he was a member of the group and perhaps we should sit down and talk! Oh, God! But why not? "The journey of a thousand miles begins with one step." To say I was scared is an understatement; I was absolutely terrified. What was I getting myself into?

We met at a quiet restaurant several days later and talked for hours. And so my education began. There will always be a soft and special place in my heart for that man. He is the one who first gently—and sometimes not so gently(!)—helped me push open that heavy closet door, a little at a time, and look out. He comforted and protected me until I was ready for what I saw. It was as if I had a second chance to lose my virginity, and it was even more significant than the first time. This time I had maturity, understanding, and resiliency on my side. I could, at any time, have walked away from it all. I chose to stay. I'm still there.

That TV broadcast, by the way, is still used in many sexuality classes as an introduction to SM. I've seen it recently, and it is still a powerful and informative show. The only difference now is that I know almost everyone in it!

First experiences in SM are difficult and can be dangerous, both physically and emotionally. The better one knows one's partner, the safer the experience will be. Most people in the SM world are brought into it by friends and lovers. Often a couple begins experimenting together, then later seeks out the organized SM community.

My story in that regard was somewhat different because I began my pursuit alone. Because of that fact, the time this man and I spent together before any intimacy developed was both valuable and necessary to develop the trust that is a key ingredient in SM play.

When we knew each other better, we established a sexual relationship, keeping the lines of communication open as to likes and dislikes. Had he not turned me on, the path could easily have been a dead end. But he did. Additionally, I now gratefully realize, on a "technical" level, he knew what he was doing; there *is* an art to SM—and to all sexuality really—and experience is the only teacher.

So each time we met, he would embellish our sex play: a scarf over my eyes here, a little spank there. He was always sensitive to my reactions, and because they were usually positive, we went on.

I was incredibly turned on, ready and willing to learn more. I liked it. Oh, yes, I liked it! Just thinking about the last time would get me wet again; thinking about the next time was even more exciting.

After some time had passed, we were beginning to "play" with "toys" (the term used for SM equipment such as whips, crops, restraints, etc.), and he suggested we attend a party sponsored by the group I had initially tried to contact. I agreed to go with certain conditions: He couldn't let go of my hand, he couldn't leave me alone even for a second, and I didn't have to DO anything or even TALK to anyone! Was I scared? You bet.

That Saturday, I barely got through the day. When he picked me up that night (what do you WEAR to a party like this?), my hands were shaking so hard that he had trouble keeping his word "NEVER to let go!" A kiss for luck, ring the doorbell, walk in.

It was surreal. I was in the living room of a lovely home. There were two floor-to-ceiling carved-wood columns separating the room into two conversation areas. Standing stretched and tied between the columns was a naked woman. One man was using a whip on her back, another was caressing her breasts with a soft fur glove. ("Get me OUT of here!" I said. "Stay put," he said.)

Once I could take my eyes off that scene, I noticed that there were about twenty-five other people in the house in various stages of dress and undress, casually sipping wine and talking as friends, as if they were regular people! It was quite a picture. I was at a loss for words.

To make a long story shorter, we relaxed with some wine, wandered around the house watching some "play"—that's what it's called—where appropriate and talking to some of the people. They all seemed so nice, so friendly and so "normal." At some point during the evening, the hostess approached me, as she had several times to make sure that I was okay (she knew it was my first time), and said, "See, we don't all have cloven hooves!"

She was right. So I began there fifteen years ago and have continued to learn, becoming more and more entrenched in the SM lifestyle. Many of the people from that first party are still good friends, and I have learned how important friendships among SM people are. We have all known the terror and isolation that come from being different and knowing it; we have all experienced the failures and frustrations that came when we first stepped out of the dark closet; and we have all known the joys and contentment of finding the place where we belong. We share a similar past, a common present and an exciting, pioneering future.

While I grew up feeling different and very alone, I never knew there was anything specific missing from my life until I found SM. Then, a void I never knew existed was filled, and I cannot imagine returning to a life without it. SM is more than just sexual activity; it is a part of who I am.

It has not always been easy. It has, on occasion, been as agonizing as it has been exhilarating. Sadomasochism has been called the "last taboo" and participating in a fringe group—especially a sexual fringe—goes against everything most of us were taught about appropriate expressions of sexuality.

By playing with SM, by learning to trust and to voluntarily (as a submissive) abdicate my personal power, I become more aware of the power I do have. Once in touch with this strength inside me, I can act on it, use it, build from it. Life in the SM world engenders honesty, a sense of self-worth and self-power, a greater degree of tolerance for other's lifestyles and a deeper understanding of human sexuality and its options.

4

Getting There
Down the Yellow Brick Road*

I remember when I was about twenty, I was working at a job where I had lots of free time to read. I had gotten a copy of a book called *The Story of O* (a classic of SM literature, although I did not know that at the time) and was reading it at work. Soon, I literally *had* to put the book down because it was becoming increasingly difficult for me to breathe. My heart was pounding so fast it was frightening. I was turned on by the sadomasochism I was reading about and that frightened me. It took many years to become comfortable with that experience, but I have never forgotten the intensity of the fear and excitement I felt.

▼ ▼ ▼

At first, many of us are understandably confused by the situation in which we find ourselves. We know we have very strong desires toward something that is considered abnormal and sick by society. We think we know the kind of activities that might satisfy those urges, but this fulfillment, more often than not, is still in fantasy form and largely outside any practical experience we've had. And we are unable to foresee just how, or even if, this could work out in reality.

My experiences (and those of my friends) have been that there seems to be two major plateaus in establishing an SM lifestyle. Both are difficult because the taboos are so very strong.

_____

*This chapter was written and edited by JJ Madeson, and the use of the term *we* is meant to indicate that she is speaking as a member of the SM community.

First, I had to admit to myself that I had an interest in this experience and a desire to act on it. Second—and this was almost a year later—I reached a stage where I could face myself in the mirror and say, "Yes, this is me, and it's okay." Of all the people I have known who are involved in SM, each one has, at some point, questioned; each has asked "Why am I doing this?" or "What's wrong with me?" You wake up the next day and say "God, it's such a turn-on—but why?"

These first steps are tough. Whether yours has been a life filled with SM fantasies (my "significant other" remembers SM-type fantasies and dreams from age three!) or these fantasies take shape later in life as it does for most, stepping into the world of sadomasochism is terrifying. For ahead lies the fear of being different, the censure of society in general and often that of family and friends. There, too, you must honestly face all the myths you have ever heard about SM: rape, mutilation, perversion, pain. Only experience and education can demystify SM and diminish the fear.

The second step—that of becoming okay with SM, of handling the guilt, of committing yourself to an acceptance of these desires as part of your own sexuality— is probably the hardest. Along the road to this acceptance, you need strength to face the fears and the guilt and overcome them. You must prepare yourself to accept the consequences of doing something that others see as very wrong, perverted, and totally unacceptable. And even if you succeed, there is no guarantee of peace and happiness—which is true of any lifestyle choice, of course.

It is during this phase that those whose interests in SM are sincere often enter the organized world of the SM community, if they are lucky enough to live in an area where such exists. On the positive side, such a community provides a social network that helps its members realize that they are not "freaky" or perverted, and, most importantly, that they are not alone.

I knew early on that if I accepted SM as a part of me, my family and friends would need to be kept in the dark, so my security in and commitment to this lifestyle had to be strong enough to overcome the loss of friends, to maintain a secret "other life," and to endure all that goes with being different. I still fight the battle of "to tell or not to tell" and am never completely satisfied with the result of that decision, whichever way it goes.

Once self-acceptance was complete, there was, for me, a third plateau that can—but need not—be reached. I call this third stage the Point of No Return. It occurred when I found that I did not wish to sustain a long-term or permanent relationship without SM. This realization was not something I worked for; it just happened.

Introducing SM into "straight" dating situations is always difficult and scary. Reactions vary, but in my experience, most are unable to handle detailed or pointed discussions about SM when the subject becomes more than just interesting conversation.

The negative aspect of this was that it automatically limited my social and sexual life to those involved, interested—or at the very least, nonjudgmental—about SM. My many friends in the community more than make up for the loss of most "straight" friends. Much more could be said on the advantages of dating those already involved in SM, but a lesbian sadomasochist summed it up best in the title of a short story in the book *Coming to Power*: "If I Ask You to Tie Me up, Will You Still Want to Love Me?" Now I know the answer will be "yes." Or better yet, "When?"

Perhaps others are more comfortable, or lucky, in finding willing and compatible SM partners. Most newcomers are brought into SM by lovers or friends already involved. If the "straight" partner is willing to try what is being suggested and finds it fun and exciting, sharing with and learning from an experienced partner or friend makes the self-identification process far simpler. It often enhances the relationship between the partners as they become closer to one another by sharing deeper intimacies.

Some people will pursue their interest in SM no further than a few pleasurable variations within a traditional relationship. Others will embark on an odyssey of sexual discovery that will lead to an even more SM-involved lifestyle than mine. Some will be more frightened and inhibited than I was. Others will explore SM with no qualms and will be completely open about their exploits, unconcerned about how their friends, family or society might react. And some will experiment with SM and simply not like it.

Each person in the SM community has made his or her own decision about how far to go down this, "the yellow brick road" of discovery. This is about the problems, issues, and decisions they encountered on the path from self-awareness to acceptance, and finally to involvement in sadomasochism.

SELF-AWARENESS

One of the reasons that sadomasochism is so difficult to understand is that the desire for and the expression of sadomasochistic sexuality runs contrary to some very deeply ingrained social conditioning. The fear surrounding SM focuses on its major departure from at least two culturally accepted equations about sex:

Sex = genitals/penetration(intercourse)/orgasm/reproduction; and Sex = tender, soft, and gentle.

We define the process of self-identification in our context as an individual's recognition of his or her sadomasochistic desires, followed by acceptance of and comfort with this "categorization."

Considering the depth of the fears, myths, and taboos about SM, it is easy to comprehend the personal strength necessary for budding sadomasochists as we strive to accept desires too strong to ignore against enormous moral, social and psychological odds. We are swimming against a strong social tide in a society that places much emphasis on image and material achievement in its concepts of identity. There is in sadomasochism, we will admit, a deliberate and conscious transgression of social/sexual taboo, and it is through this process that we define our self-worth.

When one talks with those involved in SM, various stories emerge as to how and when they recognized that SM was a turn-on. While most don't recognize or acknowledge SM interests until well into adult life—the early thirties seem to be average—some had fantasies at early ages that they are only now able to identify as SM in nature. One man, now age sixty, recalls day dreams and fantasies at age three or four where he would visualize battles between prehistoric monsters. He always saw himself as the loser, a huge animal beaten into submission and humbled by an even larger one. It comes as no surprise that this man's chosen SM role is that of submission.

Hindsight being perfect, of course, many of us in SM are now able to recognize the significance of the dominant or submissive roles we chose to play in childhood: The young girl or boy, for instance, who always wanted to be the one captured and tied up while playing "cowboys and Indians," or:

As mentioned earlier, a 1980 public television documentary called "SM: One Foot Out of the Closet" was a powerful force behind my entry into SM. Many friends and lovers with whom I've spoken identify this program as a road sign on their own journey into SM.

Many of us found sadomasochistic images in books, magazines, films, or videotapes that piqued our interest. SM images are even more frequent in popular culture now, from the leather "punk" look to

Madonna's photo essay, *Sex*, to the spectacular photographs of the late Robert Mapplethorpe.

While there are a variety of opportunities and clues by which some of us are able to identify our sexual desires as specifically sadomasochistic, at the beginning, most are not so clear on the "categorization" of such desires.

> Sometimes my husband will come home, throw me on the bed and we'll make love for hours. I have 12 orgasms and really love the rough part, but that's not SM. After all, we're not into whips and chains!

▼ ▼ ▼

> When I was a graduate student, I was talking one day with a professor about my interest in SM, and she was giving me all the standard lines about how SM is "sick" behavior, etc. But by the end of the conversation, she was saying, "Well, gee, my husband sometimes spanks me with a ping-pong paddle while we're doing sexy stuff, but that's not SM. It's just fun." As we talked further, I found that she also very much liked being grabbed roughly during sex. But that's not SM either, right?

The people described in these passages have never recognized their behavior as SM; and so indeed, to them, it is not. Were someone to suggest that these activities were actually sadomasochistic in nature, it is possible that they would abandon this type of pleasurable sex play.

Another common reason for hesitation to identify as a sadomasochist is that SM is widely (but incorrectly) seen as a pathological illness, and acknowledgment of such sexual desires does not come easily. Some fear to identify themselves as sadomasochists even if they know their sexual activities are sadomasochistic in nature, fearing condemnation from others, loss of friends and strained relationships. Sadly, these fears are often validated.

While self-identification as a sadomasochist is not imperative, the process can be a positive one, enabling us to bring together a frighteningly diverse, often disorienting, long-term, and very personal combination of desires, feelings and emotions into a recognizable and definable form.

Almost all of us with such desires once believed ourselves alone in the world; it is a lonely, scary feeling, and indeed, the main purpose of the SM community is as a support network, alleviating these fears and overcoming the loneliness. The opportunity to meet others with similar desires and experiences and share our fantasies and customs without fear or shame can be a freeing one. The desires may still be "weird," but we are not alone. That knowledge is our greatest source of strength.

I am a hard-head and resisted accepting my sadomasochistic urges for a long time. But eventually, I was able to accept them as a valid and natural part of me. It was scary; it was like a great door opening onto the unknown, but I opened it and have never looked back.

▼　▼　▼

Your body will tell you whether or not you are turned on by SM. Listen to it. If, beneath your fear and discomfort, there is arousal as well, there is an SM component to your psyche.[1]

We recognize, usually with some trepidation, the impact of these things on our own lives, and often, a significant piece of the puzzle of our sexuality falls into place.

BEING THERE

Whether you are fantasizing dominance and submission without doing it, or doing dominance and submission without naming it, coming out into SM means your conscious acceptance of dominance and submission as a key to your eroticism. You are then far more open to knowing yourself in greater depth.

The term "coming out" first sprang up in the gay community to explain the process by which lesbians or gay men began to share with others the fact of their homosexuality, a form of self-recognition. Whether homosexual, bisexual, or heterosexual, most of us know that SM is not universally accepted, and so coming out is a risk.

While discussions with friends about a newfound interest in sadomasochism is common, it is also dangerous. Almost all of us have lost friends because of our interest in SM. Our former friends, like the vast majority of the public, are frightened by what we are telling them. They do not understand how such a "perversion" can be so appealing and will wonder about the kind of person we have become; they see SM as "sick," "weird" or "perverted." Whether they have the courage to express these things directly or not, we may—and often do—lose a friend. This is a sad fact, but one with which those of us who embrace sadomasochism must come to terms.

Coming out to relatives or fellow workers is also difficult, for such relationships are more intimate (in the former case) and more structured (in the latter). Bitter experience has taught many of us that silence is golden.

> When my mother came to visit me in San Francisco several years ago, I showed her the myriad people and lifestyles in this unique city. We drove past transvestite hang-outs, leather bars, gay hotels, and lesbian gathering places. She was fascinated. Later, though, she said that while there was so much to do and try here, "If you ever get into whips and chains, I don't want to know about it." I heard the sincerity in her voice and knew that, however lightly it was said, she meant it. I didn't like that, but she'd made herself clear, and to avoid risking familial alienation, it is just easier to keep my lifestyle quiet.

Some of us have lost jobs because of a party invitation inadvertently left on a desk or being spotted in the street in SM garb. Sometimes it's more direct: We confide in a coworker, sensing a friend and wanting to share. The result is often the same: We find ourselves out of a job. Conventional offices do not want "perverts" working for them. It is, sadly, that simple.

> I learned to keep quiet at work about my personal life the hard way. A fellow secretary overheard part of a phone conversation I was having with an SM friend and reported it. A week or so later, I was fired for a non-specific reason . . . but I knew. Now, even though I talk to friends while I'm at work, I never discuss anything even remotely related to my SM life. Never.

> ▼   ▼   ▼

> While I was on vacation, someone in my office needed something from my computer. By accident, he stumbled upon an essay and a letter I had written for an SM magazine. I had meant to put a computer-lock on the document but forgot. When I got back from vacation, my boss had a "little talk" with me about keeping my personal life out of the office, and everybody else looked at me funny for quite a while. I was very embarrassed.

The secrecy of an SM lifestyle is part of the package. It is also the reason why so many of us belong to organized groups; there, at least, there is no need for secrecy or subtleties.

There are other obstacles to the process of coming out, most of which stem from the stereotypical social expectations about sexual roles. As we've noted previously, most people, men and women alike, have their first SM experiences in the submissive role; submissives continue to substantially outnumber dominants among experienced players as well. Sexual submission, however, carries with it many negative images for both men and women.

For men, voluntary submission is viewed from the outside as "wimpy," weak, even comical. He must overcome the fear of discovery by "straight" males, and his internalized version of these judgments. If the man is in a heterosexual relationship, his female partner may also have issues with his submissive role:

> When we first played, my lover was dominant with me. I knew that he had experience being submissive and wanted to share that side of himself with me, but I was frightened. My stereotype of "macho" men was deeply ingrained, and I was afraid that if his submissive persona was "wimpy," I would think less of him. I didn't like these thoughts, but there they were. Being mostly submissive myself, of course, didn't seem at all weak; so I admit my thinking was contradictory. As I came to know him better, though, the socially expected behavior roles became less important. Eventually, I just boosted my courage and approached him as a dominant. As it turned out, "wimpy" was hardly an appropriate term. His submission was loving and sensitive, and he grew stronger in my eyes. I saw a softer side to his personality emerge, and it added to, rather than detracted from, the fullness of his being. And sharing both sides of him made us closer.

Women who wish to experience a submissive role, on the other hand, must reconcile that sexual role with her feminist views and her larger role in society. Being submissive, especially to a man, is seen by many as the ultimate defection from the dignity and stature that are the goals of the mainstream feminist movement.

> According to my feminist friend, my sexual play "perpetuates the stereotype of the man as dominant and as the aggressor." In a way, she implies, we're responsible for all the sexist attitudes towards all women. I find her arguments really frustrating.[2]

> ▾   ▾   ▾

> I see the feminist issue as one of politics rather than sexuality. My politics are separate from my sexuality, and so my SM has nothing to do with my political beliefs. Apples and oranges.

> ▾   ▾   ▾

> SM is not sexist. Sexism tries to *impose* dominant/submissive roles according to our physical sex organs. In SM, we *choose* our roles

according to our own inner fantasies. Many feminists disapprove of SM, we know, but nearly all sadomasochists support the feminist movement.

In truth, the most common thread for feminists in the SM community—and there are many—is the belief that the ability to choose, whether submission or dominance or both, is part of the personal freedom they seek.

GAY AND SM: THE SECOND COMING (OUT)

Coming out is a journey people take from the straight world where they start into the gay or other variant world they want to occupy. Most of us are born and raised by straight families, educated in straight schools, and socialized by straight peer groups. Our upbringing does not provide us with the social skills, information, or routes of access into non-conventional sexual lifestyles. We must find our way into those social spaces where we can meet partners, find friends, get validation, and participate in a community life which does not presuppose that we are straight.[3]

▼ ▼ ▼

Passage into the gay world involves the acceptance of one's nature. Passage into the leatherworld involves confrontation with the elements of taboo, power and instinct as well as sexuality.[4]

There is a particularly difficult coming out process into homosexual SM, called "the leather scene" in that community. Both gay and lesbian SMers say that coming out "in leather" was harder than coming out as gay. Perhaps this is because SM is still less acceptable to society-at-large than homosexuality; more evidence that SM is, indeed, the "last taboo."

Even more difficult and hurtful is the rejection of "leather" men and women (gay or straight) by the homosexual community itself. Contrary to popular stereotypes, most homosexuals are inconspicuous, well-integrated in their professions and communities, and traditional in their social values and lifestyles. Even after gaining increasing acceptance in mainstream America, many homosexuals view the "leather scene" as too visible and too shocking, too easily used by their political enemies on the Far Right.

Not surprisingly, perhaps, but too often, even those on the sexual fringe denigrate the behavior of others in their same group.

Sexual diversity exists. Not everyone likes to do the same things, and people who have different sexual preferences are not sick, stupid, warped, brainwashed, under duress, dupes of the patriarchy, products of bourgeois decadence, or refugees from bad child-rearing practices. The habit of explaining away sexual variation by putting it down needs to be broken.[5]

Indeed, as explained by Geoff Mains in *Urban Aboriginals*,

Despite the more general acceptance of homosexuality in our modern culture, sadomasochists are poorly accepted by the gays. Their secretive institutions and relatively closed culture [are] misunderstood, and mainstream gays often take little time to investigate before they comment. To many, leathermen are seen as aloof, dangerous or sick, and leatherspace, murky in the distance and intimidating at the portals, seems safe enough fodder for attack.[6]

Thus, those who are both homosexual and sadomasochistic often must go through the coming out process twice, and once is difficult enough for most. The process is even more wrenching for lesbians, because the most radical feminist politics and the most virulent anti-SM attitudes are concentrated in the lesbian community.

My second coming out has been much more difficult than the first. The SM community is even more underground and harder to find than the lesbian community. The routes of access to it are even more hidden. The aura of terror is more intense. The social penalties, the stigma, and the lack of legitimacy are even greater. I have rarely worked so hard or displayed such independence of mind as when I came out as an SM person.[7]

▾ ▾ ▾

Yes, some of us have come out around SM. It started with fear, excitement, perhaps elation, and then a quest to find others with whom we could share concerns or discuss issues. The process reads like a feminist road map in consciousness-raising, but this time, it steered straight into a collision with a large part of the "lesbian-feminist community."[8]

▾ ▾ ▾

[SM] lesbians find themselves in a particularly difficult situation. They are treated as sinners and outcasts by the women's movement, many of whom argue that it is impossible to be lesbian-feminists and sadomasochistic at the same time, and if lesbians have been difficult to their leather sisters, gay men are rarely much better to them.[9]

Fortunately, lesbians who were coming out in SM in the 1970s had support available through Samois, an organization specifically for lesbian sadomasochists. Formed in San Francisco in the 1970s by Pat Califia (one of the most well-known and respected names in the SM community countrywide), the organization became a respected voice in the SM community with its publication of lesbian SM literature: *What Color Is Your Handkerchief?* and *Coming to Power*, a compilation of SM essays, fantasies, and discussions on various topics that, although mainly by and about lesbians, makes fascinating reading for anyone interested in SM. These books and the organization itself worked to counter the misinformation about SM prevalent in the mainstream feminist movement. Samois and its progeny have contributed greatly to broadening the horizons of women today, especially those of us who share our SM lifestyle, and we are grateful for their courage.

THE END OF THE YELLOW BRICK ROAD

Clearly, the decision to become involved with SM sexuality is a complex and emotional one. The issues, problems and dangers can seem overwhelming. Yet, those who have gone down this yellow brick road seldom speak about its hardships; instead, they rhapsodize about its pleasures. The problems and issues simply melt away like snowdrifts in the heat of SM sexuality.

> I said that I was ready, and people took me at my word so very quickly. With little conscious effort on my part, my life became a kaleidoscope of new friends and play partners.
>
> I'd never experienced my sexuality so directly or intensely before. I was in touch with my fantasies all the time. I stood taller, spoke more powerfully and laughed with a deep roar in my throat.
>
> I'd wait patiently for the next SM event, needing to be in the midst of that energy, pawing the ground with impatience. There were a thousand things I could and should be doing: See old friends, clean my apartment, read, exercise—but I didn't do them—not if I had the opportunity to experience that heat.
>
> I was discovering that SM, at least as I was feeling it, required enormous strength and stability. If I'd been more scattered or neurotic, the energy could literally have torn me apart. There's only so much intensity that the unprepared mind can take— beyond that is the realm of gods and demons—and I was rapidly accelerating towards

my limit. I reluctantly realized that I couldn't play with every person I felt attracted to, at least not that month!

Fortunately, I'd been taught discretion very early. I was playing almost exclusively with veterans of the scene. My personal life was getting very intense indeed, and I could confide its totality to almost no one.

Subtly but inevitably, I was being incorporated into the community. Viewed as if it were happening to someone else, the process made perfect sense. People in the group began to ask if I was an orientee or a member; they asked if I was playing yet; they bitched and gossiped in my presence. "Fragile—Handle with Care" was evidently no longer stamped on my forehead.

I can't pinpoint the day or the partner or the program, but at a certain point, I stopped coming out. From then on, I was just out.

$$5$$

Building Blocks
*Trust and Consent**

There are two basic concepts which, above all others, define and guide the sadomasochistic lifestyle: Trust and consensuality.

TRUST

It takes a lot of trust and courage to submit voluntarily to a whipping, I think, or to kneel at another person's feet in true humility. But I believe it takes considerably more trust and courage to acknowledge that one wants to do so in the first place.

▼ ▼ ▼

What do we do in SM? We learn to trust: Whom to trust; how to trust; when to trust. Because without trust, we are in danger.

▼ ▼ ▼

Some of my best friends are lovable dingbats, somewhat flaky but fun. But I wouldn't do SM with them. In SM, we need to trust our partners; bottoms especially need to trust their tops. Trust is like the brakes on your car: Without them, you can't drive. Without trust, you can't do SM.

---

*This chapter was written and edited by JJ Madeson, and the use of the term *we* is meant to indicate that she is speaking as a member of the SM community.

Trust is arguably the most important ingredient to each and every one of us in the SM community. By that we mean trust not just in the relationship established between partners, but that which has been built into the structure of the SM subculture itself. It has been noted that a concern with one's reputation within the subculture and the recognition that this may affect the consequent availability of partners may serve to keep behavior within acceptable bounds.

In order for SM to be safe, we must trust each other because we are playing here with bodies, minds, and emotions in a way more intense and more deeply intimate than in many other types of sexual activity. We are crossing physical, mental, and emotional boundaries, pushing and exploring limits, and none of this is possible without trust.

Trust is an absolute essential. To build valid trust requires a willingness to risk and some common sense. Since SM is consensual, there's always some talking, before, after, and sometimes even during play, so that you both (or all) know what's going on. It's a lot easier to trust when you've discussed the things that you want or don't want out of the experience, and you can relax, knowing your boundaries will not be accidentally crossed.

▼   ▼   ▼

It's very rewarding for somebody to come and say, I trust you so much that I will let you do whatever you want with me. That's not something that people say in other parts of their lives—their straight lives. In fact, our straight lives usually consist of building walls between individuals. Well, I see SM as a way of breaking down the walls; it requires total honesty, and that takes trust.

▼   ▼   ▼

You can never take for granted there's gonna be someone around who'll play safe and not cause real damage. I mean, in the real world, there's plenty of truly damaging and abusive experiences available to any willing masochist. But the fact that I would let someone whip me, someone I know I could trust not to really hurt me, but someone who would do it with care and sensitivity, with technique, with control, and who would enjoy doing it—that is both an incredible gift to give and a privilege to be given.

▼   ▼   ▼

SM is an exchange of gratification. I think SM done properly is both people working at what they're doing to make the other happy. SM to me is an exchange, first and foremost, of trust, and then of respect.

SM has been called "power exchange sexuality," signifying that the submissive partner gives up all personal power (the responsibility, care, and feeding of one's self) to the dominant. The dominant partner accepts this gift and, in exchange, assumes power over and responsibility for the well-being of the submissive for whatever period of time they have negotiated. This is an immense exchange.

> As a dominant, I have a tremendous amount of respect for the people that I dominate, because they are allowing me to do what I want. Giving someone that trust is one of the greatest gifts that anyone can give or get. "I am putting my life in your hands. I trust you that much."

▾ ▾ ▾

> [This] exchange of power is a truly balanced exchange. One cannot receive more than one is willing to give. The prerogatives are commensurate with the responsibilities willing to be assumed.[1]

This exchange is made safe in SM play with safewords* (discussed in chapter 8), respect, consent and caring, but the development, appreciation and depth of trust is all-important.

It is easy to say of a friend or lover, "I trust him." But with complete responsibility for your physical safety? With your emotional stability? With your very right to draw a breath? (Remember the words in the "Love Letters" at the start of this book: "Do you realize, little one, that in my own sadistic way, I can take away your right to breathe?") The line between fantasy and reality, "game" or not, grows fainter, and without trust (and skill), such play is dangerous.

> I suspect that many relationships are kept viable by tacit agreement not to explore too deeply, not to know one another (or themselves) too intimately. SM calls for a higher standard of trust and communication than most relationships; this may explain why so many people fear SM: they have never trusted anyone that far.

An interesting example of the parameters of trust as used in the SM subculture was noted by M. S. Magill in his 1982 study on heterosexual SM when he observed mistresses exchanging "slaves" (usually in private clubs or party situations), when the mistresses were known only

---

*A *safeword* is any one word or series of words used by the submissive during SM play as a signal to the dominant that there is something that needs attention, most often a health or safety issue.

to each other by reputation. This can be done because, within the fantasy, these "slaves" are considered property, and the trust, therefore, is not between the slave and the mistress to whom he or she has been handed over, but between the slave and his or her OWN mistress, whose judgments are trusted implicitly. The primary relationship thus takes precedence over whatever "fantasy game" is being enacted.

Trust is defined in the dictionary as "faith" and "reliance." Reliance, in our context, means the knowledge that the dominant knows what he or she is doing; and faith that he or she will not—and indeed, does not truly want to—cause real damage. This kind of trust is the foundation of all SM relationships.

It's intimate sexual connection and openness that I want, but sometimes, this stuff scares the hell out of me and I resist. But that's part of the scene, of course, to refuse until she gets through my defenses.

Sometimes I cry from being overwhelmed at the power of that fusion of physical sensation and emotional vulnerability.

And I trust my lover not to leave me in pieces, not to use the SM that we do as an emotional weapon against me. I trust her to take care of me, and time has shown that trust to be well-placed.[2]

▼ ▼ ▼

The degree of control that people show in SM, the degree of consciousness, self-control, self-knowledge, and self-acceptance, the immense degree of care and trust shared with another person—these are very intimate qualities. And I see in SM play that, even though maybe they are just beginners taking a few fledgling steps, they learn to trust more and more each time, and they handle it all with beauty and joy, caring and concern. For that person to dare to do such an intimate kind of communication makes a beautiful experience.

▼ ▼ ▼

Since I am not interested in permanent damage, when my dominant holds a knife to my breast and threatens to cut off my nipple, it is an exciting fantasy. But if I do not trust him, if I cannot rely, deep inside myself, on the fact that he will not do it, that it is just fantasy and we both know it, then the scene—and indeed the relationship—is not working, and I may be in trouble. But with the trust that we've grown to have in each other and to make the scene more exciting, we must both believe at the time that he will do it. If we don't consciously believe this, the scene is not real. It's that fine line between illusion and reality, fantasy and fact.

▼ ▼ ▼

To me, trust requires knowing that the dominant has limits, too, and that he or she is well aware of his or her own limits; it is relying on the fact that no one is going to bypass limits, and that, while pushed occasionally, the limits will be respected. Trust is the safety net.

▼ ▼ ▼

What I've found with SM is a way to tap into something deeper than just thrills; to tap into a deeper space within myself and with other people. You get very intimate with people in SM, and in a way that is not just physical. When you take somebody on an SM trip, you really have to trust both your partner(s) and yourself, and they have to trust you. You really have to listen to that person. It's a much more intimate exchange, I think, than straight sex. You really have to trust them to allow them to tie you up and to hurt you. You have to be secure that they know what they're doing.

▼ ▼ ▼

CONSENT

Clear, informed and verbalized consent is a moral dividing line between brutality and SM; partners must voluntarily and knowingly give full consent to SM activity before it begins.[3]

It's that simple.

The issue of consent, of whether SM activities are consensual or not, is a clear one to every sadomasochist. While nowhere else in this book will we speak directly on behalf of the sadomasochistic community in total, here we will:

We have chosen to do these activities, we have chosen the people with whom we share them, we know what we are doing, and what we are doing is consensual. Period.

Why on Earth
Do We Do This Stuff? *

Why? Because it's fun, it's safe, it's sexy, and it makes me feel great.

▼　▼　▼

All my life, I've hidden things about myself from myself, and all my life, that hiding has been serious business. Now, one big secret has been freed. All the emotional and physical energy that once went to shore up its defenses has been freed with it, and that freedom is refreshing, intoxicating, enlightening and fun.

▼　▼　▼

I look up to her stern face, see the pleasure in her eyes. I am drunk on the sensations I am experiencing. There is no today or yesterday or tomorrow. There is only now, and my body is ready to explode with pleasure.

▼　▼　▼

I feel safe. I [am] among friends, their silent participation adding to my security and pleasure. I can let it all go. With immense relief, abandoning all dignity, care, and responsibility. I submit to the whip. And like a bird in flight, free of the earth's pull, I soar.[1]

▼　▼　▼

SM enables me to confront the world and people I have to interact with in extraordinary ways. By releasing a great deal of the tension and stress I've carried with me my entire life, I gain energy. I feel

---

*This chapter was written and edited by JJ Madeson, and the use of the term *we* is meant to indicate that she is speaking as a member of the SM community.

empowered to say no to unacceptable behavior; I don't let anyone get away with abusing me any more. SM has provided me with the ultimate assertiveness training, not to be found anyplace else. I have gotten better at distinguishing who I can and cannot trust so I make saner choices in all my relationships.

So far, we've looked at the WHAT, the WHO, and the HOW DO WE GET THERE. We come now to the WHY.

We begin by acknowledging that human instinct, potential, ability, and pleasure are far more varied than many of us believe. Add to that the knowledge that SM is an exploration of human creative and erotic limits, giving its advocates experiences which are profound, cathartic, ecstatic, and spiritual.

As this is one of the shortest chapters in this book, some may think it odd that more space is not devoted to the ultimate question of WHY we do this. The reason is, rather than exhaustively expounding as to WHY we are a part of this lifestyle, we believe the reader has seen and will continue to see, in the passages from the sadomasochists themselves, that almost every descriptive word they use goes to the WHY.

> In SM the exchange is a mutual one, where both players give and receive erotic intensity. The trust and openness of the bottom, for example, is a constant turn-on to the top, even though it's the bottom that's being had! The power and erotic exchange always flows full circle. If it doesn't, then it's not satisfying. And the satisfaction of all concerned is a prime goal in SM.

For those of us who accept SM as our sexual preference or "lifestyle," the world we have entered is an important, deeply moving and highly personal one. The energies and emotions we experience seem obvious even to those few outsiders who happen into it and are able to view it with sensitivity rather than judgment. One such outsider, Michael Rosen, a San Francisco photographer, gained entrance to the SM community while preparing his first book of SM photographs in 1986. He interviewed his subjects in depth, photographing actual SM play, and was able to understand the emotions his subjects expressed about their SM lives. The result, *Sexual Magic: The SM Photographs*, is a sensitive black and white study of the world he saw, with written narratives by those he photographed. His own introduction articulates best what he learned:

Here, then, are the SM photographs. Photographs of Sexual Magic. Photographs of Dominance and Submission, of Sadism and Masochism, of giving and receiving erotic intensity, of giving and receiving pleasure, of role-playing and role reversal. The participants are having fun. They are turned on. This is sex play and a journey of self-exploration.[2]

The central reason that most of us become involved in SM is that we find it pleasurable and erotic.

For me, SM is about emotion, the erotic tension between my impulse toward something and my resistance against it. Every action, sensation, sound, piece of clothing, word exchanged, makes me hyper-conscious of who I am.

▼ ▼ ▼

When we play, when we're doing whatever it is we choose to do, I always feel that there is almost an electric connection between us. It feels as if there were an arc light that flashes back and forth between us, a sharp, narrow laser beam of high energy current and fun that shoots between his body and mine and back again. I feel his energy, his passion, his love, as if it were traveling through an electric wire connecting us with the power on full blast in both directions. It's sharing so very much.

▼ ▼ ▼

My pleasure and passion pour out of me directly to her, even as her pleasure and passion flow back to me. Back and forth. Back and forth. Her love, my love, her joy, my joy.

▼ ▼ ▼

We are hiding nothing; we are truly sharing everything that we are deep down inside, and the shared feelings are so strong and loving, it's sometimes overwhelming.

▼ ▼ ▼

It's like ESP. I know—I feel—in my mind with total certainty that she's having as much fun as I am, and she knows the same. She feels the same. It's a wonderful exchange of joyous, sexual energy that's palpable.

SM is an exciting, exhilarating experience, enabling us to feel a deeper sense of ecstasy or sexual satisfaction than we ever achieved in "straight" (or "vanilla") sex.

My experience is that SM has given me so much confidence and knowledge of my sexuality that there's always a quality of SM in my lovemaking.

▼ ▼ ▼

One of the differences I find between SM sex and vanilla sex is because, so often in the latter, each person is concerned primarily with his or her own satisfaction and the lover's needs are met only as part of a payment or trade-off. In SM sex, each partner seeks to open as much as possible, to push past limits, to turn each other on so intensely that there is no possibility except full satisfaction, not just physically but emotionally and psychically as well.

▼ ▼ ▼

In SM, sex becomes a musical instrument with its strings tightened, raising the key to a sharper and clearer sound. Sharper: the tingling is no longer centered on genital orgasm, but can involve sensation and release throughout the body. Clearer: an intense interchange of communication, trust, openness and caring is part of every SM experience.

▼ ▼ ▼

For me, sexual intensity is heightened as we enact deeply held fantasies, experiment with role-playing and role reversal, exercise and exchange power, and explore and challenge our abilities to experience pain, pleasure and other sensations.

Sociologist Gini Scott, another "outsider" who spent some time "inside," states in her book *Erotic Power:*[3]

For some, this intensity yields an extremely profound, extremely intimate, and sometimes even spiritual experience in which they come into touch with their own deep feelings and those of their partner. [SM] offers them not only immediate sexual satisfaction but a lingering spiritual or psychic fulfillment. They speak of a blissful surrender in which they communicate with their partner in an unmediated mental or physical fusion in which the pleasure the dominant gives and gets and the submissive receives become intermingled.

And insiders say:

When I cry sometimes after a scene, it's out of love, out of a feeling of gratitude. I'm very, very happy for what we're doing. I'm happy for the intensity; I'm happy for the pain; I'm happy that my partner

lets me be submissive; and I'm happy that she wants to be dominant—
and with me! SM goes as deep as my soul.

▼ ▼ ▼

People just don't realize that it's such a natural high. No drugs, no
alcohol. And believe me, it's a higher high than any kind of drug
could give you. It's extremely spiritual. It involves skill, sensitivity,
a kind of psychic awareness and, basically, it's grounded in sexuality,
which is always fun!

▼ ▼ ▼

We are exploring new realms of creative sexual expression, and SM
satisfies certain fundamental psychological needs like the experience
of power and control (for the top) and the experience of giving up
power, and release (for the bottom). It's a sexual interchange creating
a profound closeness, intimacy, and a deep sense of communication
and trust with your partner, allowing personal growth.

▼ ▼ ▼

Playing this way, so erotically, has given me a lot of power in the
everyday world: To be more tolerant, less covert, and to ask for what
I want instead of having to be manipulative and cute in order to get
what I want. I don't have to manipulate anymore; I just accept who
I am and I associate with others who accept me as I am. I am thus
much freer to express my own desires and needs.

▼ ▼ ▼

I'm very picky about the people I'll top, and I want my submissives
to know that I am watching them very, very closely. That is where
I find the pleasure in being dominant: watching my submissive get
pleasure from the things I'm doing which gives me pleasure in return.

▼ ▼ ▼

SM has really helped me to be more myself, to love people more and
be more tolerant. I think if we in society could put our violence and
negativeness and desire to oppress in a safe, consensual, erotic outlet
like we do in SM, the world would be a much better place.

▼ ▼ ▼

We have bypassed some of society's taboos, along with attendant
guilts and anxieties, and have come to recognize our self-worth. There
is little need for status in this world of SM, and while titillation can
provide enjoyment along the way, the ultimate purpose of SM is not
to titillate but to gratify on a personal level.

▼ ▼ ▼

Above all, SM gives me the opportunity to know and love myself. I explore all sides of my personality. I get joy from being a bully, a tyrant; I get a perverted sense of security from being the "victim" of someone I trust. SM provides me with the space not just to tolerate these things about myself but to celebrate and admire and learn from them. There is freedom and power here, and I am grateful to be a part of a place and people who respect all of me.

▼ ▼ ▼

I have grown so much. Sadomasochism has shown me the strength and depth of my personal power by playing with it—whether by exaggerating it as a top or giving it up as a bottom. I am clearer on my own sense of self so I can be more effective in other areas of my life. Playing in the SM arena has allowed me to be more direct in my personal life.

In researching her book, Gini Scott observed:

To an outsider observing SM—the whips, the ropes, the ritualized insults, and so forth—this kind of inner experience may be hard to imagine. Yet we are clear that an inner transformation occurs through the combination of intense physical, mental or emotional stimulation.

Some describe profound personal changes that result from their [SM] activity: The discovery of new qualities in themselves, a heightened awareness of their own power or ability to submit, and the experiencing of a deep sense of communion with another person. For some the experience is almost a mystical or spiritual transformation.[3]

And again, insiders say:

I've been involved with SM for two years, and I believe it has freed me to explore a wide range of inner thoughts and emotions, previously unexpressed, and integrate them with my outer, more public face, making me stronger as I interact with others.

▼ ▼ ▼

I had struggled with and mostly suppressed submissive feelings for many years. Now that I'm out, I have found an emotional intensity in my relationships that I had never experienced before, and this intensity has become an integral part of my life.

▾ ▾ ▾

I've found that SM has really helped me get rid of a lot of passive-aggressive shit and communications problems. You really learn how to be clear about what you want and that it's all right to want ANY-THING that you want. I think a lot of misunderstandings and not hearing each other and not being brave enough to be honest get burned away in SM. It's in the nature of the situation that you become more honest and courageous.[4]

So the range of WHY is as varied as the participants and the activities themselves, and regardless of status in life, acts of sexual submission and dominance in the context of sadomasochistic play allow that the cares and worries and responsibilities of the everyday environment can be set aside along with the business suit. A new and fresh perspective can be gained. Much like the worker who goes to the gym every evening for a strenuous workout, sexual play and its aftermath have a profound effect on one's attitude toward oneself and toward others. In SM play, as in any other kind of sex play, there is a welcome transition from the tensions of social and economic responsibility of life to a state where frustrations and negative feelings can be put aside in a satisfying and pleasurable experience, where anxieties diminish and one can feel a surge of new energy.

It feels good to let go of the struggle for a time, to just relax and give up all claim to power or decision making. It's like a drug high without the drugs. I don't care if it's endorphins or whatever. I come out of playing stronger and more secure than I went in.

▾ ▾ ▾

SM is the only time I'm only paying attention to one thing.[5]

▾ ▾ ▾

We spend so much time immersed in a society (whether business or otherwise) where we are controlled by forces beyond our control, where we must behave in a prescribed manner for a prescribed time. How wonderful to go into SM play, giving ourselves the opportunity, whenever we want, to act out the emotions and desires and fantasies that we are constrained from even considering "out there."

▾ ▾ ▾

To release all the pressures of all the things considered inappropriate or immature or just plain wrong, to do the things that we usually suppress or even hide (even though we want to do them), it just feels great.

▾ ▾ ▾

When I've had a terrible, frustrating day where everything that can go wrong has, the idea of coming home to submit to the whip (or to wield it) is so delicious that it even makes that awful day a little easier. She strips me, ties me down and whips me everywhere. I scream and yell and cry and let it all go. Wow!

▾ ▾ ▾

SM means that I can act out different fantasies and wonderful things happen to me. It's deep, almost spiritual. I get a feeling of fullness in myself and in the power I have in life. It makes my life feel more real sometimes just knowing that power is there. I'm more confident, more sure of myself, sure that I can handle anything. That's very real!

▾ ▾ ▾

How is it a lifestyle? Whether physical or mental, I do it and live with it every day, and it's very much a part of my life.

▾ ▾ ▾

The realities that are shared between us, whether through pain, prolonged bondage, or heavy acting, have a profound effect on subsequent actions in the larger world, making us better able to deal with tensions and limits and appreciate some of the real impulses that underlie behavior.

▾ ▾ ▾

Let's be clear here: I do this because it's terrifically intense when we're doing it, and afterwards, it feels like—have you ever watched a cat stretch? It feels like that! So utterly content. And that's why.

Roles
To Have or Be Had:
That Is the Question★

WHAT'S IT REALLY LIKE?

The following story, which concludes on page 90, was written specifically for this book. It will, we hope, give the reader a clearer idea about what goes on in the minds of the participants during actual SM play. The point of view in this story is that of a heterosexual male dominant and a female submissive because the author is a heterosexual male Top! But the feelings and emotions described here could just as easily have any other orientation.

Grant's Tale: The Beginning
BY GRANT MORGAN

Terrified butterflies beat in my belly, and I felt as if I'd never seen the bedroom before, for tonight I looked upon it through eyes that were wide and timid. Sweat slicked my armpits even as anticipation trembled in my blood, my nipples throbbed, a hot trickle of arousal oozed down my thigh, and there was too little air in the room. I seemed to hang on the brink of hyperventilation, filled with a singing sensuality, an anxiety dark with forbidden excitement and soft with trust.

I licked my lips as I turned to face him. His eyes were different, too, dark not with the coppery-tasting anxiety in my own but with fiery, predatory tenderness. Perhaps that sounds insane, for how can someone be both lover and predator? Surely one must be a mask for the other, the lover only a ploy to lure the sweet-bodied fly into the

---

★This chapter was written and edited by JJ Madeson, and the use of the term *we* is meant to indicate that she is speaking as a member of the SM community.

spider's web. Yet it wasn't. I knew it wasn't. We'd discussed this too many times in the year since he'd told me of his fantasies.

They'd terrified me at first, those darksome dreams of his. They'd resonated deep inside me, echoing and reechoing with all the tales of men who abused women, or rape and worse. Yet even as I'd feared them, something had called to me, and another something—something which came not just from me, or from him, but from both of us—had mocked my terror. This was Paul. My lover. The gentle man who treasured my pleasure as his own and celebrated my wanton, sensual side with his lips and mouth, his tongue and hard, sweetly demanding flesh.

Yet he was also the man who dreamed of owning me. Of confining and compelling me. Of rendering me helpless, obedient to his will. He hadn't pressured me. He'd simply told me, then said no more until *I* asked *him*, begging him to explain how he could want to be both lover and owner, how he could love me yet long to make me less than him. The questions had hung in my brain, demanding answers, and even more than *his* answers, I needed my own. I needed to understand why the thought of *his* dreams should gild my own with fire.

But I already knew my answer—in part, at least—for I, too, had fantasies. Fantasies in which I *was* helpless, constrained, impotent, forced to experience the fire of my own desire and answer to another's. I'd always tried to ignore them, for they'd frightened me. A modern woman wasn't supposed to feel such things, not supposed to *want* to yield to another's control, become his silken plaything, and I'd sensed a dark, brooding danger in their seductive power. A sense that if I ever once yielded to them, it would change me forever.

I feared them still. That was why I sweated, why my mouth tasted coppery. Yet their dark allure was what brought me here this night and lit the fire in my blood, for he'd answered my questions. "Trust," he'd said. "It's all about trust, Suze. About you trusting me enough to *give* me control and me proving worthy of *being* trusted. It's a game that *isn't* a game, a fantasy that becomes real—but only for exactly as long as we both *choose* for it to be real."

And so I'd come here, and now I licked my lips once more and cleared my throat.

"What do you want me to do?" I asked softly.

I stood in the doorway, drinking in her beauty and tasting her tension. Her nipples puckered her blouse, and bright streaks of fire burned high on her pale cheeks as she brushed back long black hair with one fine-boned hand. There was fear in her brown eyes, but it was overlaid with trust and desire, and a terrible tenderness filled me.

The decision had been hers. I'd described my desires to her honestly—as honestly as I could—for I loved her. Yet just as I knew she didn't fully understand the reason she'd agreed, I knew I didn't fully understand why it was so important to me that she do so. Oh, I knew many of the reasons, and I suspected others, but some of them go so deep, are so fundamental a part of me, that I've never been able to lay my hand fully upon them. I'd told her it was about trust, and it was. It was also about commitment, and passion, and the pleasures of the flesh, but there was more. A part of me truly *did* want to own her and make her fully and completely mine. To subdue her, control her, *possess* her. Yet it was important—essential— that *she* want that, too. That she yield to me of her own will, reaching out to share a tenderness the world did not understand and refused to condone. That we create our own private, secret world, where no one else ever came, and take off all our masks. Prove to one another what we truly were, what we truly desired, how deeply we truly loved. And as her willingness to be made helpless proved her trust, so must I prove worthy of that trust, never harming her, never abusing her faith in me. What happened would be up to me, for I would be the initiator, yet even as I hungered for her supple beauty and the wet, slick clasp of her flesh, I knew I must also be certain I *remained* in control . . . not simply of her and of the game but of myself.

"What do you want me to do?" she asked softly, and I smiled and knelt to open the trunk. I heard her breath hiss as she saw the straps and ropes at last, and I looked up at her.

"Take off your blouse and jeans," I said quietly, and she swallowed and reached for her buttons with a tiny, spastic nod.

My fingers trembled as I unbuttoned my blouse, revealing my sheer bra, and let it slither from my shoulders with a shiver. The air-conditioning was cool on sweating skin, and my panting belly jerked as I unsnapped my denims and peeled them down. My panties tried to go with them, and I felt myself flush crimson as I stopped and tugged them back up. It was silly. Paul had seen me naked more times than I could count, knew ever intimate inch of my flesh, yet this was different. I'd stripped for him before, teasing him with my body to make him want me, yet never like this. Then it had been my decision; tonight it was his. *My* only decision had been to come here and do whatever *he* commanded, and I felt small and fragile and afraid.

Yet even as I felt those things, I was aware of a new and deeper power. The power of impotence. The fierce desire my submission woke within him. I stepped out of the denims and stood before him, clad only in wispy, smoke-sheer lingerie, and smelled my own lust. I was lost, lost, wandering into some decadent, beguiling dream, yet even as I floated powerlessly into the waiting void, I sensed my own dreadful importance, for *I* was what the dream was all about. I was its core, the honeyed fire burning at its heart. *There can be no master without a slave,* a voice murmured deep inside me, and I flinched in dreamy horror from the thought. "Slave." "Master." Paul hadn't used those words. He'd said "submissive" or "bottom," just as he'd said "dominant" or "top," yet *I'd* thought them. And as I did, I recognized the truth of my own fantasies at last, the desire to let go, to abandon myself. To surrender the responsibility of control and become simply me—the sensual, debauched, gloriously wanton me I'd dreamed of being, absolved from all inhibitions. And I could, I realized, truly *could* be absolved from restraint, for if I gave myself to him, he could *compel* me to do all the things I'd never been able to compel myself to do, and because I was compelled, I could abandon myself to them without limit.

I kicked the denims aside, put my hands at my sides, and looked at him, and this time I didn't speak. I simply stood there, waiting, while a furnace roared within me, and every nerve ending sang and crackled with unbearable sensitivity.

Her brown eyes were huge, darker and deeper than the sea, and sweat dewed her brunette-dusky skin. The dark wedge of her crotch silk was a bold shadow through her thin panties, and snakes of passion wept down her thighs. She didn't say anything else, and I realized she wasn't going to—that her silence was an announcement. She'd said everything; now her mute, shuddery waiting was her sole message, her confirmation that she was truly mine and trusted me to create and orchestrate the moment. I opened my mouth to tell her how much I loved her, to promise once again never to harm her, to try to say how deeply I treasured her gift of herself. But I closed it again, for she already knew those things. Her knowledge quivered in the taut silence between us and echoed in her deep, urgent breathing. It would have been wrong to tell her again, as if I felt she needed to be cajoled, tempted, *bribed* into this to "buy" my love. She had no need to "buy" anything from me, and the suggestion that she might would only cheapen the gift she'd given not because she *had* to but because she *chose* to.

I finished selecting my restraints, stood, and crossed the rug to her. Her eyes clung to the leather as I laid it out on the dresser, and then she swallowed, nostrils flaring, as I gripped her slender shoulders. They felt fine-boned and fragile, her skin hot and smooth as satin, her muscles quivering with tension, and I turned her gently to face the bed, then pulled her arms behind her.

His hands were huge on my shoulders, his fingers long enough to reach clear down to my collarbone. He was a tennis player and a runner, tall and rangy, not lumpy with muscle, but I'd always loved his strength, the masculine power of him. Yet I'd truly never felt that power before tonight. I'd known it was there, relied upon it to lift things far too heavy for me to move, but I'd never *felt* it this way, for it had never occurred to me I might someday find myself in his power. And as the strength of those hands turned me with gentle, restrained potency, I realized something else. If he's ever tried to *make* me do this, I couldn't have stopped him.

The awareness hit me like a hammer. He was a foot taller, and far stronger. Whether or not he had a *right* to take me, bind me, force me—*hurt* me—he'd always had the *power* to. No doubt it would have destroyed our love if he had, but that didn't mean he couldn't have done it.

And he hadn't. Oh, we'd argued and quarreled like any other couple, said hurtful things and then made up tearfully, but not *once* had he tried to *force* me to do anything. Convince me, argue me into agreeing, lose his temper when he thought I was pigheaded or stubborn, yes, but never had he attempted to *make* me agree, concede . . . surrender. And in a way I knew I could never define, that made everything all right. No less scary, no less passionate, but all right. The fact that he'd never before given me cause to fear his strength or size kept me from fearing those things tonight, for my surrdner was willing and passionate, not a thing of compulsion.

He drew my arms behind me, and I bit my lips, hips rolling as a fierce spurt of fire crackled in my belly, as leather touched my wrists.

I buckled the leacher about her wrists. I'd chosen extra-wide straps, for this was her first time, and my responsibility to take care of her— *for* her—was an essential part of the complex alloy of my own needs and emotions. I would confine her, render her helpless and *prove* to both of us that I had, but I would do so cautiously, alert for her responses and the message of her reactions. There can be tenderness in giving pain, in wringing tears from the one you love, but only when your lover wants that, too. The fusion between a bottom and a top is more intimate than anyone outside it can fully comprehend, but if it is not based on consent, on *sharing* and mutual desire, it becomes corrosive as poison, and I would not—*could* not—let that happen to my and Suzy's love.

I drew the strap tight enough to squeeze firmly, pinning her slender wrists together. Her breathing quickened still further, and I heard a soft, wanton groan—one of passion, not hurt—and my eyes widened in delight. Few people can touch their elbows together behind them without pain, but Suze only panted and trembled with passionate anxiety.

Strain curdled my shoulders as he fused my elbows. I sensed the care he took, how slowly he went, ready to stop if he hurt me, and my inner thighs quivered as excitement stuttered in my nipples and belly. I felt my petals swell, wet and glistening while I pouted and shook my head in slow, dreamy passion. It *did* hurt—a little—but it was good hurt. It was a welcome pain, hovering in the cocoon on my eroticism and making the cocoon hotter and sweeter by its very contrast.

He reached to the dresser again, and I whimpered hotly as the collar went about my throat.

I buckled the collar snugly. It was a wide collar, closed with half a dozen small straps and tall enough to force her regal head fully erect. It pressed the underside of her jaw, the leather thick enough to punish her if she tried to lower her head, but I took care to be certain it didn't bind.

▼ ▼ ▼

I fastened the last collar buckle, then slid my fingers slowly down her strapped arms and over her hands, caressing them and feeling for any coldness, any sign her circulation was affected. She moaned, rolling her head, hips jerking in small convulsive arcs, and I leaned forward to kiss and nip her shoulders gently. She whined, and I smiled. She's always been a noisy lover, my Suzy. She's exuberant, giving voice to the passion inside her, urging me on, and I've always treasured her sounds of pleasure. But tonight they were deeper, throatier, darker, and I slid my right hand back up her arms to grip the sable silk of her hair. I wrenched her head back—not harshly, but implacably, letting her feel my strength and her impotence—and my mouth crushed down on hers.

I cried out into his mouth as his lips devoured mine. He'd *never* kissed me like that! It was hard, fierce, demanding, ruthless. His tongue battered at my teeth, forcing them apart like a conquering army, and my own tongue roused to meet it. They mated and twined in liquid fire, yet it was *his* fire, not mine. I answered to him, responded, reacted, but he initiated and controlled, and my knees buckled. I panted wildly through my nose, shuddering and twitching, afire with a rawer, more elemental *hunger* than I'd ever felt before, and all he'd done was *kiss* me!

I don't know how long that kiss lasted, but when he broke it at last, I felt myself sag. I was melting, slagging down into the wet furnace between my legs, and my closed eyelids fluttered as he traced my wet lips with a fingertip.

"Open," he whispered, and I obeyed, then gurgled in strain as the gag wedged home.

I'd replaced the harness gag's rubber ball with one which had never been used before and bored a half dozen holes through it to be certain she could breathe. I'd tried to gauge it to fill her mouth completely without being so big as to be painful, but I'd mis-estimated a bit, and she groaned and twitched as it forced her jaws wider than I'd intended. Yet she made no effort to escape it. She only strained her jaws still wider, accepting the imposition of my silence, and then gasped in relief as it socketed home behind her teeth and her jaw muscles relaxed slightly.

I shuddered, panting even harder, my terror suddenly sharper and brighter as the stretchy hurt swelled my mouth. In many ways, the gag was symbolic, for I knew all I had to do was hum three times and Paul would remove it instantly. I *knew* it, for he'd insisted on the signal himself and I trusted him absolutely . . . yet trust was my *only* assurance. I could still make sounds, but I could no longer speak. I couldn't even *ask* him to stop, and the theft of my voice diminished me somehow, made me *truly* helpless, for there was no way I could compel him to return it to me. That knowledge blazed within me, confirming my impotence, making it *real*, and for a moment, I could no longer breathe at all. I writhed in a burst of panic, gurgling as he buckled the straps, webbing my head in leather. But the panic passed as air whistled through the holes in the gag, filling my lungs, and I moaned and went still once more, trembling as I absorbed the totality of my plight . . . and the fire in my blood.

▼ ▼ ▼

I fastened the last buckle. I'd sensed her panic and been ready to remove the gag, but I'd also sensed the moment that panic eased, and I smiled tenderly down at the top of her head. I reached around her, squeezing her breasts through her sweat-soaked bra, and she arched her spine and crooned deep in her throat, pressing her nipples against my palms and grinding her bottom against my fly. I felt my own hunger, my need, and I wanted her. I wanted her right then, right on the bedroom rug. I wanted her gasping and shuddering under me, grunting in strain as I plundered her gagged, strapped body. I wanted her crying out in passion, exploding as my seed erupted deep inside her, filling her, sealing her with the badge of my possession. But this was her first time, the beginning. There would be time for that later, when she knew what to expect and could respond with all the wanton delight we both could desire. For tonight, I must go slowly, exploring her limits and proving my fidelity by respecting them.

There was one more touch needed, and she whimpered as I fitted the blindfold over her eyes.

I whimpered in primal fear as the padded leather stole my sight as the gag had stolen my voice. I felt him buckle it, fixing it immovably in place, and my skin twitched with sudden, unbearable sensitivity. I could no longer see. I was trapped within my own body, sealed into a mute, sightless void where only my passion and the touch of his hands on naked skin was real. Blindness drove me inward, forced me to focus on what I could *feel*, for that and hearing were the only senses left to me, and that made every instant a singing eternity of tension.

My darkest fantasies had never prepared me for the reality of this moment of complete and utter vulnerability, of total impotence . . . or for the jagged tide of passion lashing through me like a whip. I was a flower, an erotic rose blossoming under the dark sun of his power, and in that first instant of blindness, I saw myself through *his* eyes, realized how much sexier, how much more wanton my helplessness made me. In an indescribable way, I *shared* his power over me, for I'd given it to him, and at last I truly understood how he could be lover and beloved predator in one and how both parts of him could be equally real, equally true. He was two people, and *I* was two people, for just as he had become my lover and— yes—*master* in one, *I* had become his lover and *slave* in one. And because it had been my decision, because he'd never tried to force it upon me, my "slavery" made me a queen, my helplessness my crown. Perhaps that sounds crazy, but if I was mad, it was with a joyous, fearful, exultant madness that filled me with passion.

I trembled, and then he hooked a finger through the ring on the front of my collar. He pulled, gently but irresistibly, and I whimpered yet again as I followed obediently. I couldn't see. In my blindness, each step became another stride into the dark unknown, one I took trusting him to lead me aright and keep me from falling. I was totally dependent upon him—for guidance, for safety, for ultimate freedom, for *everything*—and the dependency that burnished home my impotence fanned my passion to crackling heat.

I led her to the bed, then sat, and she trembled uncertainly, unable to know what I intended, as I moved her between my knees. She stood facing me, arms behind her, and I reached up, gripped her bra, and jerked.

He ripped my bra away, and I whined shrilly, hips jerking as a mini-climax whiplashed through my belly. It was a small thing, perhaps, after all he'd already done, yet it was also enormous. Somehow the rending of my lingerie was a declaration of his power, his authority. I was *his*, and he would unwrap me, bare me to his possessing eyes and touch, however he chose.

I trembled, panting in the aftermath of spastic pleasure, then groaned and threw my head back, arching my collared throat, as his mouth found my breasts. He stalked my nipples, clasping them between gentle teeth and lashing them with his tongue, and even *that* was different! His tongue was harsh, demanding, almost cruel. It flogged my pleasure buds, crushing them against the unyielding hardness of his teeth, taunting me with his power and control. It hurt—a little—but there was so much *passion* in the hurt! Such a terrible rush of eroticism! I groaned again, snuffling through my gag, pressing forward, urging him on, and felt his soft chuckle of delight vibrating into my tender flesh.

He kept it up forever, yet he stopped far too soon, and I moaned in disappointment, trying to lean still further forward, mutely begging him not to stop. But just as the choice to begin had been his, so was the choice to end, and I sobbed in passionate frustration as he took his mouth away at last.

I stood between his thighs, panting, sweating, blind, burning, and then gasped again as he turned me and bent me over his left thigh.

She folded elegantly over my thigh with a gagged, wanton groan, blind head lashing, and I laughed. I peeled her panties down, and her thighs parted eagerly as my right hand probed between them from behind. She was hot and wet, her passion oozing into my palm, and she gasped and bucked wildly as I found her clitoris. I touched it with exquisite gentleness, but she squealed into her gag, head flailing, and I withdrew my touch. She sagged back, head dropping, panting over my thigh, and then grunted and jerked again as I slid two fingers up inside her.

The touch of his hand on my clitoris was unbearable. I was too aroused, too sensitive. I hungered for his caresses, *needed* his touch to drive me over the brink into orgasm, yet even as I craved it, it *hurt*. But he took his hand away, and I moaned in disappointment and relief, then grunted and bucked as two fingers slip up inside me. They moved within me, filling the air with their wet, slurping, sucking sound, and I groaned. He was neither rough nor cruel, yet neither was he gentle. He was measuring me, evaluating his possession. I knew it, yet it was his *right* to pierce and probe me, to set the seal of his ownership upon me, and I clenched my muscles tight.

I smiled as her muscles rolled my fingers in a hot, wet vise. Her bottom twitched and her thighs clasped my wrist, sealing my hand against her. Her hips moved, stroking as she made love to my fingers, and I felt the tremors of approaching orgasm shudder within her.

But it wasn't time for that—not yet—and it was not my hand which would bring it to her, and so I withdrew my fingers. She moaned once more, shaking her head, thrusting her pelvis against my thigh to beg for their return, but I wiped her honey on her sweating bottom and closed my legs. I clamped her thighs between mine and gripped her strapped wrists, lifting them high behind her with my left hand while I cupped my right across her buttocks.

I tensed as he clamped my legs between his and raised my arms, bending me still further over his thigh. I felt him cup my bottom and whimpered in sudden fear, and he laughed softly.

"I'm going to spank you now, Suze," he whispered. "I'm going to spank you hard. It's going to hurt—at least a little, possibly even more than that—but I won't harm you. Do you understand the distinction?"

I whimpered again, biting the gag that swelled my mouth with silence, and felt my bottom tense spastically. I hadn't been spanked since childhood, and then it had only been an occasional swat for some misdeed. Now I was a grown woman, and he wasn't going to punish me. He was going to spank me simply because he could. No, he was going to spank me to *prove* he could. To prove to both of us that my submission—and his power—were real.

The thought of being spanked was both humiliating and frightening. Humiliating because I *was* a grown woman, not a child, and frightening because I'd finally realized how strong he truly was. I knew he *could* hurt me, just as he'd promised—even worse than he'd promised, if he was careless—and I was gagged. Would he even *notice* me humming for release? If I did, how could I tell him he was spanking me too hard? How could I make him *stop* hurting me if he hurt me too much?

I couldn't tell him—or stop him. The thought was terrifying, yet it was also necessary. I knew there were far more . . . strenuous things he might have chosen to do, and I already sensed that I would sample those more strenuous things on nights to come. But this was my Rubicon. This was the moment in which I would accept his right to punish me, however lovingly, as the proof of his possession. And by accepting it *knowing* I couldn't control what happened, I would also let him prove I could trust him to do those more strenuous things, trust him to know his strength and my limits.

"Do you *understand*, Suze?" he repeated quietly, and I nodded.

She nodded, the movement of her head spastic and afraid but definite, and her strapped hands clenched into small fists. Her bottom clenched as well, as if it could somehow escape my palm, and I smiled. I knew she could feel the iron of my erection against her belly, knew she was afraid, felt her eagerness warring with terror, her passion foaming like a tide over the rocks of anticipated hurt. I knew—as she surely suspected—how much hotter and fiercer her pleasure would be when I finally took her, when I finished spanking her, finished wringing the diamond tears of submission from her, and strapped her spread-eagled on the bed to plunder her with slow, sweet arrogance. In a sense, that pleasure was what this was all about, and I wished it could last forever. It couldn't, of course; it was too intense, and neither of us could have endured it if it had, for it was special. The moment of true acceptance, that crystal instant, snatched from the heart of time, in which our adventure truly began. There would be other moments, special in their own ways, but never again one like this. I bent to kiss her bottom lovingly, and raised my arm.

▼ ▼ ▼

Tops think bottoms are the sexiest people alive and vice versa! So you choose: Dominate or submit? Top or bottom? Would you rather have power over a highly erotic person or would you rather BE that highly erotic person someone wants to have power over? It's a win-win set up.

▼ ▼ ▼

SM is putting up with a picky, uncertain submissive, novice-new, who doesn't know how to say what he wants to say; but when he finally says it, he takes your breath away with the totality of his submission.

▼ ▼ ▼

Submissives and dominants were interdependent parts of a whole, a partnership in exploring sexuality.[1]

There is vast diversity of people, styles, and possible activities in the SM world and the activities we do, how we learn to do them, and what we gain from doing them are limited only by our imaginations: Virtually limitless.

For most of us, it is the dynamic between the dominant and the submissive partners that provide the context for the entire SM Experience, and these roles, therefore, are the most significant component of our SM play. While there are those who enjoy the physical aspects of SM activities in and of themselves, the majority of us see the dominant/submissive interaction as the foundation of the SM Experience.

During SM play itself, and in order to make it "work," the Top and Bottom must share patience, humility, an openness to learning, a willingness to communicate and the honesty to express ourselves at our most basic level. This sharing creates a strong bond between us, and the result of intense play is a deep purging and release of tension in an ongoing search for erotic pleasure.

Simply put, both dominance and submission in SM play are, more than anything else, mental attitudes. To put it in context, there is some dominance and submission (sometimes called a "power exchange") in every relationship, be it sexual, personal, business, or otherwise. The truth is that we all role-play and, in some situations, are actually required to do so: the child, for example, must behave submissively toward the parent, just as a parent is expected to behave dominantly in the relationship with the children.

Another obvious example is in business, where the boss is the dominant, holding the ultimate power to end employment. As anyone in the business world knows, it is necessary for those who are NOT in charge to maintain a submissive attitude toward those in power, whether or not one actually feels submissive, because financial and personal security is at stake. If you are but an employee, your attitude must be one of submission, of giving in to the will of another. This may or may not be a totally voluntary attitude, but to keep a job, it is often necessary.

> How much more rewarding in this world fraught with tensions of role-play [employee/employer], of self-definition, of ongoing probing, to let loose in a scene where all is done for affection and for pleasure.[2]

Indeed, the same power dynamic exists, for example, between teachers and students, in military ranking, between husbands and wives, and sometimes even between friends. There is almost always one who is the Top and one who is the Bottom at any given moment. Whether we are talking about decisions of where to go on vacation or what to serve for dinner or deciding who will be the initiator in a sexual encounter, the one who makes the decision is, for that time, "on Top."

Further, since there is no hard and fast rule as to who will play which role, this power will often switch from one to the other and back again, depending on many things: the topic under consideration, the superior knowledge or stronger feelings of one over the other on that subject, the depth of caring about the outcome of the process or, many times, one's feelings about the process itself.

In the sexual realm as well, this power dynamic holds true, and in some ways who's on top or who's not is far clearer here than in other situations. Sexually, someone must make the first move, whether by physical action, verbal innuendo, attitude or some other means, and the person who makes the initial approach is, at least at that moment, the Top. But once again, the power here can, and often does, switch back and forth between the partners in a split second.

Physically, who's on top, figuratively or literally, seems obvious, but that does not take the attitudes of the partners fully into account, and it is the attitudes of the participants to the encounter that come into play in sadomasochism.

Regardless of an individual's position in "real-life" (sometimes I wonder which is "real" and which is not)—whether they have control of six hundred people in the workplace or are one of those six hundred; whether one is a teacher and one a student; one a private and the other a major—one's sadomasochistic role is a well-thought-out, practiced and very deliberate choice. In fact, the dominant or submissive roles adopted in the course of SM play are often quite different from an individual's "real life" role. This common occurrence is the basis of the stereotype of the bank president who leaves work, goes home, strips off his pinstripes, and voluntarily submits to the whip of his partner.

> Everybody has different persona. You have a business persona, a friend persona, a family persona and a sexual persona. If you look at any group of people in a business setting, you don't have any idea what they are like in their bedrooms or anywhere else. It's as irrelevant to their business persona as what they're like in church or what they're like with their parents.[3]

Since the SM Experience itself is the expression, sharing and enactment of sexual fantasies that most frequently focus on the theme of one person having power over another, it is imperative that the true equality of the partners be suspended and replaced, for the duration of the play, by the illusion of inequality. This illusion forms the basis of the interplay between the partners and is characterized most effectively as a "power exchange" (where power = control of and responsibility for) wherein the abdication of personal power by one and the assumption of that power by the other creates two new personae: the dominant and the submissive.

> The energy, the excitement, that is created between two people satisfying each other, one in submission, giving the gift of power, and the other in the joy of being given that gift and freely using it, that's what it's all about.

> ▼ ▼ ▼

> [He] values his submissive and considers her his equal. In role, do what makes you happy. When it is time to drop the fantasy, each of you is a full and equal partner.[4]

> ▼ ▼ ▼

> Dominance and submission are really attitudes, and the head space— the attitude—is the best part. The physical things that accompany

that mindset are all good, but it's the role that makes it for me. If it was only physical and not psychological, I wouldn't be as turned on.

▾ ▾ ▾

It's a power play. But in that power play, what the submissive is doing—and here we are again, back to trust, love, respect—is giving up that power to the dominant, and the dominant is taking it, knowing it comes with love, respect, trust, and everything else, and also giving the same back in pleasure that is totally consensual. It can only be that way.

▾ ▾ ▾

As long as it's a matter of choice, and I know he really does not think he owns me, I feel secure in doing what I'm doing.[5]

SM roles are varied and complex, offering different things to different people, but the goals are the same: an intense sexual experience, fun, emotional release, catharsis.

How does SM make fantasies real? First, it frees us of inhibition. The dominant is freer to act because the submissive has freely submitted. To have a bound, helpless partner—what power! The submissive is freer because the dominant has taken control and responsibility. To be bound and helpless and able to really let go—how wonderful!

Each role carries with it different responsibilities, but both face certain psychological obstacles that must be overcome before the individual can become comfortable with the chosen identity. The main obstacle is the fear of the desire to play out fantasies that have not only been repressed for years but that, we are well aware, represent socially unacceptable behavior.

On a personal level, these roles often represent character traits that, while present in us all, usually have socially negative connotations.

For the dominant, these can include aggressiveness, cruelty, power, and control, and a desire to inflict pain. For the submissive, the desire is often to be sexually humiliated, used, hurt, and humbled.

Sadomasochists turn this negative energy upside-down and transform it into a cosmic implosion of sexual energy, shielding ourselves with trust and love. Most people survive their emotional turmoil by resolving what they can and repressing or denying the rest. We SMers are made of sturdier stuff. We give our demons free rein in the dungeon, play with them there. We expose our demons for what they are and get to know them as pieces of who we have become.[6]

▾   ▾   ▾

Being Bottom comes so smoothly to me; it's like diving into warm water. Being Top came harder to me. Power and cruelty have so often gone hand in hand in my life, and I feared that in myself, feared my own power and taking it so openly. But as I've pushed past this barrier, I've found myself claiming power with more honesty and courage than ever before in my life.[7]

Rather than deny these traits in ourselves, SM allows us to express them fully in a safe place, to "get them out of our systems," if you will, in a "mindspace" where the everyday grip on reality has been temporarily altered. We can scream and yell, protest and exhaust ourselves; if we are submissive, we can play the "Oh, no. Please don't do THAT!" game just for fun and let out all that tension. Then, when the scene is over, we are able to rejoin the everyday world energized and balanced. Thus, we return with a clearer and stronger perspective of the world around us. Some of this may sound familiar in other contexts as well, such as drugs, religious trance states, the ecstasy of dance, or the high of aerobics.

Sadomasochists have, through playing, faced obstacles directly, head-on, and have been able, despite strong social pressures and with a little help from friends and lovers, to accept these parts of ourselves. Indeed, SM's exaggeration and eroticizing of these personality traits and desires diminish the negativity associated with them.

SM is accepting the dark side, accepting totally who I am as a complete human being. I am not a wonderful person all the time; sometimes I feel really mean and nasty. Things happen in my life—and I'm sure not alone in this—things go wrong and I ache to take out my frustrations on someone. With SM, I find people with whom I can act out these frustrations by making them specifically sexual. Not in anger—never in anger—but with a grateful understanding that my lovers appreciate even these dark parts of me. That's a more complete sharing, a deeper intimacy.

▾   ▾   ▾

I finally had a way to let the masochistic side of me, which was there anyway whether I wanted it or not, exist, instead of always trying to deny and push away and be afraid of a part of myself.[8]

▼ ▼ ▼

There's a part of me that's a bitch. I think there's that part in all of us. That's not to say I can be a bitch with every one of my play partners; I can't. But I do find some who are turned on by the bitchy energy I have! With them, I can let all that out. I can be a bitch! It's consensual; they're getting what they need and I'm getting what I need.

▼ ▼ ▼

First time submissives: They're nervous; they're shy; they're scared. They've never done this before; they've heard this is bad, all that sort of stuff. So you talk with them. You take them into a room and start doing what you talked about, the whole time encouraging them to accept it, to feel it, to flow with it, and to allow the ecstasy. Nervousness may shut that off at first, so you have to actually get them from high nervousness to a relaxed state and then show them what ecstasy is in a totally different form than they've known. By sharing their inner feelings, sharing them with me, they're trusting me with their fantasies, their very souls. That's a significant gift but it's also a little scary.

▼ ▼ ▼

When I'm doing SM, I'm very present. I'm not wandering off inside my head, wondering what I'll have for dinner or some such inconsequential concern. With the intensity of SM, you HAVE to be there. As a Top, you're responsible for your bottom: You have to be focused on what's going on. As a bottom, the intensity is such that there's no way you can think about anything else; you MUST be fully present. Your bondage, whether physical or mental, ties you there.

▼ ▼ ▼

The energy I use to dominate is the energy I receive from my bottom. His submission feeds my dominance and vice versa till it gets to the point where little else exists in the world, little else occupies my mind. It's a very COMPLETE experience.

▼ ▼ ▼

I like the feeling of power, the energy flowing between us, the energy that we create together. Seeing her ecstatic, knowing that I'm responsible for that, what a turn on! I derive pleasure from seeing that I've created so much pleasure for someone else, and she gets pleasure not only from what we're doing but from knowing the pleasure she is giving me.

Let us now explore in greater depth the complexities of these SM roles. We shall begin—all puns intended—at the top!

FROM THE TOP

The point [of dominance] is to get someone to surrender her physical self to you, and, as surely as whips crack, her heart and mind will soon follow. Please take care of these three items. People are very, very fragile beings, even you tough guy sadists. Never be ashamed to drop the roles and the game when the going gets too rough and always be ready to offer a hug and a kiss to remind each other what this is all about to begin with.[9]

▼ ▼ ▼

Succinctly put, I just always wanted to be in charge. What's so wrong with that? I'm not in a position to do so in my real world, so now's my chance. And I've found others who want me to be in charge sexually. How wonderful!

▼ ▼ ▼

Slowly I realize that my feelings of powerlessness in this world fill me with a great desire to be powerful and being top does it in a safe way. I get to be powerful and someone loves me for it![10]

▼ ▼ ▼

Dear Columnist: My submissive just won't behave. She won't do what I tell her to do. What can I do? Lady Beige.

Dear Lady Beige: Order her to do what *she* wants to do. Now she'll be in a bind! If she does what she wants, she'll be following your order; and if she disobeys your order, she won't be doing what she wants to do. Soon she'll be so frustrated and bewildered that she'll be begging you, "Do something to me!" just to get out of the dilemma. Then you step in and do whatever you want. Come on, somebody ask me a hard question![11]

The dominant (or Top or Master or Mistress) is the director, choreographer, engineer, artist, in charge of music and lighting, and head of the creative department. The dominant is the one who, after discussion and planning, decides what to do, when to do it, and how. They set up and guide the journey through the fantasy that has been chosen, and the submissive follows along, but is not, as might be assumed, in any way passive.

If somebody is being real passive by just lying there and getting off on what I'm doing, it doesn't turn me on. I like the feeling of somebody really *wanting* me and giving back the sexual energy.[12]

▼ ▼ ▼

Submissive is not the same as passive, for passive means inert. Submissives, in their desire to be controlled, often provoke, resist, scream and holler and fight back. They are often great exhibitionists and love dramatic scenes! And even if their physical or verbal behavior is not obvious, the creation of the energy that flows between the partners, while not visible, is intensely felt.

The dominant's primary excitement is in the exercise and manipulation of the power granted by the submissive, as well as in the submissive's reaction to the scene.

Dominants on Dominance

When a person is kneeling at my feet, *submitting* to me, there is such an incredible feeling of power. Previous to my involvement in SM, I did not relate to the term "lust for power." I have now experienced that lust as the power of the scene surges through me like a drug, first to my crotch, then fanning up and out through my whole body. It's overwhelming and it's wonderful.

▼ ▼ ▼

I need to know who my partners are; it's very important that I know exactly who they are, what their limits are, what their talents are, what they can do, what they can't do, what they're afraid of, what they love and which buttons I can push.

▼ ▼ ▼

I always take into consideration who I'm playing with. I look at my submissive as if I were an artist; I take whomever I'm playing with and see them as a piece of clay for me to mold in any way I want. It's imperative that I know what kind of clay I have, but once I know that, watch out!

▼ ▼ ▼

I love being able to walk in the door and have him instantly drop to his knees. I love the vases of flowers that were never there before. I love playing with his obsessions. I love being a mean and unreasonable bitch. And even better, he loves those same things. His submission to me brings us both pleasure. What could be better?

▾ ▾ ▾

I would not do this if her sexual energy did not attract me. I am still exploring its complexities, watching what she fears, how she is aroused. And she, in turn, is studying me, trying to understand and match my fantasies.

Sometimes, of course, we're simply mellow and sweet. Outside of role, we're friends; we respect each other. We really do. Don't doubt that for a moment. But then, I'll rub her neck and bite her ear and she'll whimper in anticipation, and then . . .

And *Dominants on Submissives*

. . . and the sexual sweetness I find in her surrender brings on the rush that speeds from my head to my groin and back again as she gives in and gives me . . . anything.

▾ ▾ ▾

It shows so much love, his giving up all he is to me. It's a beautiful gift each time it happens. I see the look of total trust in his eyes, the look that says he'll do anything I want. It's a powerful rush; it's an exciting, intimate, sexual feeling.

▾ ▾ ▾

When I'm Top, I want to push through her ambivalences, strain her limits, and help her experience all the feelings she's drawn to, but fears. Whatever I do, whatever I say, I listen and watch her very carefully. . . . I want raw emotion, reaction, the best possible, most heightened reaction to whatever I feel might work to break through her composure and day-to-day facade.[13]

▾ ▾ ▾

If I want a seventeen-year old cheerleader, a Vegas showgirl or a hooker, that's what she becomes. I give the orders, she follows them. I create the atmosphere, she fits it. We are both actors who really get off on the play.

▾ ▾ ▾

Sometimes when the scene's all over, and I see tears on her face— that relaxed, calm, satisfied pretty face—it creates a bond between us in a way that—well, it defies description. We have shared something so intimate, so very special.

▼ ▼ ▼

When I hear my submissive scream in ecstasy or agony and see on his face and in his eyes that he's loving every second of it, I see that I've made him happy and that makes me happy. It's beautiful; it's ugly; it's terror; it's total trust; it's total contentment.

The Ideal Submissive

My ideal submissive will know the difference between strength and stubbornness, preferring the former to the latter. I don't do brats. Still, I want someone with a solid sense of self-worth. Someone who is happy being who she is and can communicate what it is that she wants. She will treasure romance and be thrilled by heady, perilous, dramatic fantasy.

Outwardly we will appear as doting lovers, even sickeningly so. Because between us, there will be such easy communication as to leave no room for argument, such dedication that one never wants for affection from the other, such commitment to each other's happiness that one never thinks to manipulate the other to satisfy personal needs. Easy communication, dedication and commitment are just manifestations of the intimacy we will share. The driving force beneath it all will be a common need, one so primal that it cannot be defined by words, it can only be alluded to by metaphor.

For at the core of my ideal beloved's sexuality will be an urgent longing to surrender to and be thoroughly consumed by a sexual beast. Because, if she is the right one for me, and I the right one for her, our coupling will be like locking battle to get outside of ourselves and into each other, always searching for the beast. With each coupling, I will lead her further along a path of discovery guided by a beacon of pain. She'll submit happily each time as I show her how to transform the pain into pleasure, using each stroke of the whip to take another step in our quest.

Then, while our passions find ever stronger release, surging and melding, drawing strength from deeper and deeper sources within us, the beast will at last rise between us, creating itself of raw intensity, heat and obsession. It will hover over us, surround us, suffuse our every straining, groaning fiber while we spit our lovers' rage from between clenched teeth. It will take control of us, tearing away the layers of virtue and morality that define us as individuals, laying bare two aboriginal souls, merged as one in a combat of primitive heat. This is the fire that feeds the beast, and in giving it life, we will bask in the light of its power. But the beast lives only as long as our bodies can sustain the tempest and when we reach our final gust of fury, its body is ripped in two, the halves sucked back into each spent lover.

Philip Miller and Molly Devon,
Screw the Roses, Send Me the Thorns

AND FROM THE BOTTOM

I can only describe the attitude of submission as that of acceptance, relaxation, and, if possible, a turning off of the intellectual process, allowing your body to respond without any conscious process, just instinct.

▼ ▼ ▼

The submissive, by accepting the submissive role, is allowed to play out the illusion of complete powerlessness. She can no longer do as she wishes, *and is thus completely free.* The [Top], in accepting responsibility for the direction of the scene, is allowed the illusion of complete powerfulness. She can do as she wishes, *and is thus completely free.* Through different paths, both parties have arrived at a feeling of complete freedom. It is only temporary, and it is an illusion, but it is very compelling.[14]

▼ ▼ ▼

She was never so feminine as when she stood beside him, sagging in his arms, abandoning herself to anything he wished, in open acknowledgement of his power to reduce her to helplessness by the pleasure he had the power to give her.[15]

▼ ▼ ▼

One of the most common types of psychological abuse we see is by the dominant who demands submission without being willing to assume the responsibilities that dominant entails.[16]

The sexual and psychological rush submissives feel is as exciting, though somewhat different, as that of the dominant. One of the express purposes of an SM scene is to make the submissive feel little or no control over just about anything; however, the truth is that "only consent by the submissive allows the dominant to maintain control. Every order obeyed is a decision to submit."[17]

Tops like the power, the control. It works so well because I, too, want the Top to feel and experience the power and the control.

▼ ▼ ▼

Submission is being open and vulnerable and incredibly trusting. It is the ultimate humbling experience. Letting go of all that you are to another for that time is so freeing. She just looks at me in a certain way—she doesn't even have to touch me—and I'm turned on.

To say that the submissive is the recipient of most of the dominant's actions during a scene is true; to say that the submissive is the only recipient is, as we have just seen, quite untrue, for SM play is a mutual *exchange* of power, of energy, of love and of respect.

Beneath most master/slave relationships, there is a strong sense of equality and mutual respect. Voluntarily adopted sexual and even social roles do not mask a deep-seated belief that, although of different capacities, the partners remain full equals.

▼ ▼ ▼

When the dominant accepts the surrender of the submissive, they together create a legend that elevates a dominant to a position of nobility. Honoring this conferred rank by kneeling, wearing a leash, foot-kissing or other seemingly abasing acts may actually engender pride in the submissive. The dominant becomes lord by his submissive's empowerment and she takes reflected glory in the exercise of his dominion over her.[18]

Imagine This

Imagine my body draped over the bed
feeling the pounding in my heart
as you stand above me
teasing me with your corrupt words.

Do I love it? Oh, yes.
But I love your sweet torture more.
The anticipation of your next action
burns in my mind.
My submissive soul is in your hands,
  and at your mercy,
    I wait.
            (August Knight, 1993)

A common social perception frequently equates submission with weakness or "wimpiness," but this stereotype vastly underestimates the power, strength, and emotions of the sexual submissive.

> The submissive in a consensual relationship does not relinquish social or professional power, nor is she likely to accept authority from anyone but her dominant. Many submissives have told us that the ability to surrender sexual power privately and to fulfill taboo fantasies is a profoundly empowering experience. . . . While submissive women often bitterly resent stereotyping as passive victims, dominant women are in a double-bind: Even if they overcome the anxiety that sexual assertiveness is unfeminine, they may then grapple with feminist theory which mitigates against any overt expression of power in intimate relationships.[19]

▼ ▼ ▼

> When I play, I truly yield to the will of my Master in the deepest way I can. I give up my personality, my own desires. Even sharing fantasies is, in some ways, giving them up. He takes everything from me piece by piece, and when it's all over, like Humpty Dumpty, it takes us a while to put me back together again and go on with life. But he's there with me afterwards, holding me tight, and that helps to make the experience complete.

▼ ▼ ▼

> When I totally bottom out, it's hard to come back to reality. I need a good top to bring me back to ground zero, to center me and hold me, because I've been flying way out there; I've given up control, responsibility, just about everything. When it's over, I'm so satisfied and tired that my body feels like Jello! It's the Top's job to finish the scene, to do what's called "closure," to help bring both of us back to where we can function independently again.

As these last quotes indicate, in order to "survive" this total abandonment of "personhood" so integral to the dynamic of the dominant/submissive relationship and be able to reclaim ego strength and self-identity fully when the play is over, requires of the submissive a strong sense of personal stability, strength of character, and self-confidence that invalidates the stereotype of weakness. As psychologist Theodore Reik stated, "a person with a weakly developed imagination [or a weak sense of self] cannot become a masochist."[20]

> It might seem that when I'm feeling weak, uncertain, when things aren't going so great in my world, it would be a great time for me to

get into my bottom space and let the outside world go away. Actually, it's just the opposite! If I come to my dominant weak and weary, the onslaught—the giving up of my ego that happens when we play—can be devastating. The alternative is for the dominant to "go easy" on me, and that's not what either of us wants. No, I need to feel strong and together, really okay with myself, to be submissive and vulnerable. My mistress doesn't want a fragile weakling anyway. If that's where I am, there's no power to give up, no struggle, and it's not nearly as hot.

So, *Submissives on Submission*

Being bound tightly, held down, imprisoned—whether physically or mentally (and it can be either)—is so secure a feeling. I'm responsible for nothing but giving my dominant pleasure. All I have to do is feel and absorb and give. My body reacts all by itself because, after a while, the intensity overwhelms any deliberate reactions. The energy that flows between us is electrifying. It's like a four-hour orgasm.

▼ ▼ ▼

We masochists are very proud people, for behind our humility and submission, we know our own strength!

▼ ▼ ▼

When the intensity of a scene has been very high, when we're too exhausted and satisfied to even talk, sometimes I cry. I'm not always sure why, but usually it's because he's really pushed me. And although it's been hard, when it's over, we feel so incredibly close. Submission is one of the ways I've chosen to show him how much I love him.

▼ ▼ ▼

What words would I use to describe the feelings of submission? Surrender. Giving up control. Freedom. There's great freedom in being a slave—especially a willing slave.

▼ ▼ ▼

It's hard for me to give up, to become submissive. Sometimes you actually have to gag me to keep me quiet, tie me up and everything else, and then I'll still fight you. But how I love the fight! If it's enjoyable to you, then okay, let's play. When it gets to that point where it's just right, I can't believe the high. What I feel is ecstasy like a continuous orgasm that comes out of every single pore of my skin and lasts forever.

▼　▼　▼

I was dominant for quite a while, and it took me a long time, many years, to come to the realization that I just do better as a submissive, and that there's nothing wrong with that; it's okay. It's not sick; it's just the way the sexual me comes out.

▼　▼　▼

Submission is flying free. Being whipped really hard and feeling as if I'm floating in the sky, I'm truly free. I have no worry at all. The rest of the world is gone; I'm just soaring above it all. Could somebody whip me too hard when I'm in that "place"? Possibly, but nobody ever has. I have to trust them, and as long as I can do that, it'll work. The whole idea is bringing more into focus the erotic self.

▼　▼　▼

In SM, we expand our facility for communication, learning to do so through the slightest quiver of muscle or the slightest touch.[21]

▼　▼　▼

The child in me is part of my submissive persona. I'm playing a "child who needs nurturing and can be punished" game. In some ways, I think submission replays our infant dependency. To be a child again, what a treat! We can test and expand our limits, be smart-alecky, deserve and get punishment and be safely cared for, all at the same time. And to be loved. So loved.

Just as dominants are picky about the submissives with whom they play, so are submissives choosy about their dominants. They look for someone they respect and trust as an equal, with whom they can be comfortable in the intimacy of play, and someone with experience and skill, for the submissive's position is somewhat more risky in terms of safety.

And so, *Submissives on Dominants:*

I belong to her, and I love that feeling. That's part of the domination, the owning. The physical act of giving my ass to her to whip is actually one of the lesser things I do in terms of total submission to her. The play is wonderful and I love it, but everyone focuses on physical acts of being bound and whipped, and there's so much more to being submissive than that. Being a good bottom for her is important to me; it is how I show my love.

▼ ▼ ▼

She tested the limits of my tolerance for pain, and explored with me my desire to serve and my willingness to submit. She took pleasure in meting out sufferings and, when I surrendered to her, took what I gave with greater pleasure, becoming even more the woman she first seemed to be. Human, available, unembarrassed, and vulnerable, she did not worry whether I'd usurp her power; she was not frightened that she might do something wrong. She knew she was big enough to hold whoever I might be, and I let myself fill the space she offered.

▼ ▼ ▼

Over the months, my Master has destroyed all thoughts of resistance with his own skillful blend of torture and affection. I became an eager slave because he made me want to please him more than anything in the world. My submission gives him such intense pleasure that I endure it willingly, even welcome it. Like when he lets me massage his feet—I still can't believe how this potentially degrading act has become a truly joyous privilege, just because of the pleasure he gets from my willingness to do it.

▼ ▼ ▼

I trust her and love her. She hurts me because we both want that; she cares for me and pushes me to do more and better. And I can surrender freely, knowing she will push me only as far as we agree.

The Ideal Dominant

The ideal [dominant] controls himself, so that he might control his submissive. He will, as a stern dominant, cause tears to flow, and as lover, kiss them away. An unashamed romantic, he cherishes his submissive lady. Yet always, he remains aware of the difference between fantasy and reality. When there is need, he is ready to leave the roles behind to be a friend.

He understands that to own a woman, one must court the mind with intelligence and humor: win the spirit with compassion and warmth; and take the body with determined strength.

He is the honorable sadist who uses pain to extend the bounds of pleasure, vigilant that no harm comes of the hurt. He is the mentor and guide who takes his lady into flight, the wind beneath her wings and her tether to the earth. Enveloping the submissive in his strength, he lends her the courage to reach new heights.

The good dominant is not lazy, mentally or physically. He researches carefully his toys of choice. He seeks out those having the skills and knowledge to teach him to use those toys properly. Then, he practices each skill he would have, whip to cane. Trusting nothing to chance, he tests everything first on his own body.

He is patient enough to learn his submissive well. Aware of the fragile nature of the human mind and spirit, he would not violate those entrusted to his keeping. He knows that submission to him will deepen as trust grows and control will extend as affection increases.

Confident in his dominance, he has no need of silly posturing. He accepts titles as tokens of respect and kneeling as outward expression of genuine feeling. He has no desire to cheapen these by compelling a ritual. He understands that the compliance that comes out of fear of punishment is weak at best, while the obedience engendered from real submissive feeling and the desire to please one's master is unequivocal.

He is secure enough to laugh at himself and the absurdities of life, courageous enough to accept assistance, open-minded enough to learn new things, and strong enough to grow. His tools are mind, body, spirit, and soul, with assistance from whip, chain and blindfold. He understands that each partner gains from pleasuring the other. Most of all, he knows love as the only chain that truly binds.

> Philip Miller and Molly Devon
> *Screw the Roses, Send Me the Thorns*

Though most SMers began as submissives, many eventually identify both dominant and submissive impulses within themselves and learn to enjoy both roles. Indeed,

> . . . experience and sensitivity count for more in SM than youth and looks. It takes years to make a good dominant or submissive, and age is an advantage. Tops who have also been bottoms are prized: They've been there and they understand.

Thus, the SM community contains many "switches" (also known as "duals," "middles" and, occasionally, as "dominissives") who can play both the dominant and submissive roles.

> Both places take a lot of energy. If feels good (sometimes) to let go of the need to be powerful and just relax, give up all claim to that power. It also feels good to claim all my power, to feel it, to enjoy it, to express it. I get to play with the incredibly different parts of myself. I get to use all that energy to feed me instead of to block me.

▼ ▼ ▼

Dear Columnist: When I go to an SM party and see an attractive stranger, how can I tell if they are a top or a bottom?

A. Offer to top them—you'll find out fast.[22]

Some believe that switches have the best of both worlds, allowing greater flexibility and creativity than one who is strictly submissive or strictly dominant. As expressed above, it is also widely believed that the best dominants are those who began as submissives, because they understand from experience the psychology of "bottom space."

> As a submissive, I once played with a partner who *ordered* me to be dominant with him. It was a unique experience, and I tried. But dominance is an attitude, really, a state of mind, and all during the scene, I still felt like a submissive *trying* to be—or being *allowed* to be—dominant. My dominance was not real; it wasn't working, and we both felt it. I guess I'll just have to try dominance when I feel ready.

▼   ▼   ▼

> I was submissive for the first few years of my SM life. I swore I would never be dominant, had no interest in being dominant and believed that I would probably giggle if someone called me "Mistress." Even if I had wanted to switch in those early years, those with whom I played were strictly dominant and the opportunity never presented itself.
>
> After beginning my current relationship, my lover (who is a switch) was interested and open to explore with me my dominant side, so I tried it a little at first, being very unsure and uncomfortable. But now, three years later, I am about a fifty-fifty switch and enjoy my dominance a lot. I guess it's a case of "never say never." Over the last few years, my submissive man has whispered, "Yes, Mistress" during a scene and giggling was the last thing on my mind. I deserved the title; I had earned it!

▼   ▼   ▼

> I like to feel both sides of SM, the different things it requires of me, the emotions it dredges up. I like the feeling of giving up control, and I like the feeling of exercising control, taking her to that edge— and holding her there. Being given such power and responsibility is as erotic to me as giving it up.

Socially, the decision for switches as to which role to play and when depends on the situation, the partner(s) one is playing with, and what kind of play is expected. If attending a male dominant/female submissive party, that obviously is the orientation for that event. Some parties are "mixed" with no specific orientation, and the roles adopted by the participants vary according to their own desires and/or relationships.

Some will even play a dominant role with certain partners and a submissive role with others.

> I'm mostly dominant, but there are times, under certain circumstances and with certain people, that I will give up my dominance for submission. At that point, it's total trust, for this is a side of me rarely seen, and I must have very special feelings about the person with whom I am sharing this play.

Privately, the decision as to role, as described by the switches, "just somehow happens."

> A handsome male switch named McBroom
> Took a young female switch to his room,
> They argued all night
> Over who had the right
> To do what, with what, and to whom!

▾ ▾ ▾

> My partner and I both switch and the decision as to who plays what role when is rarely a problem. Perhaps one of us has more energy at that particular time, so that person will usually adopt the dominant role. We've never had the experience that switches worry about: that we would both want to be submissive and have to sit around and hope a dominant shows up! It just doesn't seem to happen that way . . . at least not often!

▾ ▾ ▾

> We often switch roles several times in an evening of play, and those changes usually happen during our breaks or "safe time" when roles are temporarily suspended, and we relax and catch our breaths. Then, one of us inevitably just starts feeling dominant and the other follows as submissive. It is almost as if, during a break, we put the power on the table, and it waits there for someone to pick it up and use it. It's just another part of the Sexual Magic.

▾ ▾ ▾

> We used to switch often during play time, going from one role to another, back and forth with ease. It seems now, though, that since we play at more and more intense levels, switching is not as easy. When I'm submissive, I'm VERY submissive, and it's hard for me to switch to dominance. The "head space" and depth of my submission is deep, emotional, and quite complete. I can't just turn it off and take over.

On the other hand:

It seems that if we switch during an evening of play, it is easier
for me to go from submissive to dominant than from dominant to
submissive. Once I have the power of dominance, I don't want to
give it up and take somebody else's orders. If I start the play as a
submissive, taking up the mantle of power and taking charge is easier
than giving it all up once I have it.

On the other hand:

If switching is an option during our play, I prefer being dominant at
the start and then switching to submission. Dominance is hard work
and although submission is not exactly easy, I can relax into it if
the opportunity presents itself. I can stop making decisions and let
someone else take control for a while.

▾ ▾ ▾

Although I am most often dominant, I do find myself occasionally
wanting—no, needing—to give it all up and experience the release
of submission. It seems a matter of balance. Once my submissive
"itch" has been thoroughly "scratched," then I happily take up the
whip again, full strength and power restored.

▾ ▾ ▾

I'm dominant on occasion, but I am basically a submissive. Two of
the men I play with are very strong dominants, but they, too, are,
at heart, submissives. When they top me, it's always wonderful and
I love it. There's no question that when they're topping, they are
totally committed to their role and are fully *there* with me. But in
the back of my mind, I know deep down they'd rather be submissive.
I'd never want to stop playing with them but sometimes I think I'd
like to find a *totally* dedicated Top who has no desire to switch.

WHO'S REALLY IN CHARGE?

One of the issues often addressed by researchers, theorists, and practitioners of SM focuses on whether the dominant or the submissive
really has control of a sadomasochistic scenario.

SM has been called "power exchange sexuality," and in this context,
power usually means control or responsibility for activities, behavior,
verbalization, sometimes even of basic body functions. During SM play,
the appearance is that the dominant is in charge and the submissive is
not. The submissive turns over the control to the dominant to exercise

as he or she sees fit for a specified period of time; the submissive will do as he or she is told. This is the most basic psychological dynamic of an SM scene.

> The dominant is also a submissive partner in an SM relationship. This is because the dominant, although "in control," is in control within the physical and emotional limitations of the submissive. Both have a good deal to contribute and respect each other's ability to do just that.[23]

The complexity and contradiction lies in the fact that the abdication of power by the submissive assumes that he or she possesses this power in the first place, which, since we are talking about control and responsibility for one's self, is, of course, true. As someone once put it, "The submissive has the power to give up the power."

But if this is true, does this exchange mean then that the submissive is in charge? Dr. Wardell Pomeroy, former Dean of the Institute for the Advanced Study of Human Sexuality in San Francisco and a former Kinsey researcher, believed that it *is* the submissive who controls the scene and, often, the relationship itself.

> Having the submissive set her own limits leads one to wonder who is really running the show. Where people are a now-and-again role-play, this is a valid question. With a . . . submissive, however, an innate craving to please her dominant is strong and unquestionable. A . . . dominant also feels an instinctive need to feel in charge, yet neither can realize these parts of themselves without the other.[24]

Pomeroy suggested that the dominant is concerned (and rightfully so) with the submissive's reactions and pleasure as well as his or her own, and therefore the submissive can, by verbal and/or physical language, manipulate the dominant into doing what the submissive wants.

> I was playing at a party with a dominant I didn't know very well. At some point in our play, she pulled out a knife and began lightly scratching the skin of my arm. It was meant to be an erotic threat; she was trying to frighten me, and she succeeded better than she knew. Irresponsibly, she had used no alcohol to clean the knife, done nothing to protect me (like an alcohol prep) from an activity which could cause serious harm if not done properly. I didn't want to break the mood of the play but I needed to stop her from doing that particular activity. So I deliberately overreacted, as if she was hurting me too much. My reaction stopped her in her tracks—which was exactly

what I had in mind, of course—and she put the knife away, probably deciding that I had a low pain tolerance. That was okay—at least I stopped her.

Such deliberate manipulation in SM play does exist. In the example above, there was legitimate reason for such manipulation, but that is not always the case. As a dominant man stated, "I have been controlled by submissive women all my life!"

> As I have progressed in an understanding of my submission, I have found myself on occasion attempting to manipulate my dominant into either doing something that I want or avoiding something I don't want. This can be done subtly with body language or verbal responses. When I feel that happen, though, I make a real effort to stop. I want to be truly submissive, to do and want whatever he wants, and I must therefore work even harder to give up power and control over what happens.

Any attempts at manipulation by the submissive can be, and most often are, simply ignored by the dominant, lending credence to the familiar cliche where the masochist begs "beat me, beat me," and the sadist says "no." In the SM community, this kind of manipulation is called "topping from the bottom," and recently a new term has been coined for such submissives: SAMs or SAMmies—Smart Ass Masochists—and attention is given, with a sense of humor, to the best way of dealing with these "problem" cases! Some sort of punishment (chuckle) is certainly in order!

In truth, of course, a degree of manipulation exists in all relationships in that both partners contribute to, and each has a certain amount of control over or input into, what takes place within the relationship, whether these contributions be open suggestions or subtle hints. In this context then, the question of who is in control is more closely related to the dynamics of the relationship than to anything else.

In SM play, though, the dynamic is somewhat different. A submissive explains:

> Whether the scene lasts hours or days, the whole idea behind the role-play hinges on our agreement that I will abdicate to my Top my responsibility, my decision-making capabilities and control over my life for that time. In return for this surrender, my dominant receives and exercises total power and control over me. Our agreement contains the caveat, however, that we will not openly acknowledge the fact that this is role-playing, for to do so is to contradict the illusion

and destroy the mood. He desires the feeling of power; I desire the feeling of helplessness. In SM, we both get exactly what we want. I call it mutual selfishness!

The concept of the safeword is often used to support the position that the submissive is in charge. The argument is that since the safeword exists almost exclusively for the submissive's benefit and, by using it, the submissive can change or stop the play, it is the submissive who is in control.

But is it? The dominant has the power to explore and expand the limits the submissive may have expressed and, it should not be forgotten, the submissive often *wants* these limits pushed, whether for personal satisfaction or as a show of true submission, and is hard-pressed to use the safeword unless absolutely imperative. So both the submissive's hesitance to use the safeword and the dominant's ability to push slightly past stated limits work to add realism to the scene and enhance the all-important illusion of the dominant's complete control.

If, in fact, the bottom had most of the control, the interaction would be predictable and sexual dominance would be a farce, negating entirely both the fantasy play and the reasons for it. So I disagree strongly with those who believe the submissive is controlling the scene because I believe that both partners share equally in that control.

▼　▼　▼

More than exercising power over another, we negotiate and share power by exchanging it. Trust, respect and equal cooperation are all necessary for this erotic dance of love and power.

The significance of these issues is their contribution to the underlying equality we see in SM play, rather than supporting the view of the submissive's control. Both partners agree to play and either may stop it; nothing in SM play is unilateral because full consensuality is imperative.

This is the most equal I've ever felt with anyone.[25]

By *exaggerating* the inequality of the partners as an integral part of the SM play itself, the partners are allowed freedom from stereotypical social roles.

Further, the respect and equality inherent in SM play contributes greatly to the success and strength of the non-erotic parts of the relationships, giving them true role balance rather than role inequality.

In the eyes of the public, a sadomasochistic scene is a very sordid affair with a "sex fiend" brutalizing an equally weird "victim." It is seen as being without sensitivity or any aesthetic feeling. In fact, though, the exact opposite is true. The SM relationship, sexually and otherwise, is the most democratic that exists! The two partners must work very hard to achieve a compatible relationship because mutual respect and trust is imperative for the incredible intimacy and vulnerability of sharing deep fantasies. The successful SM scene can be compared to production of a drama composed by equal contribution from two or more authors, and a great deal of intuition, ability to improvise and cooperation is needed.

▼ ▼ ▼

At the beginning of a party for female dominants and male submissives several years ago, and before play had begun, there was a dispute over the rules of a game we were about to play, and to settle it, a show of hands was requested. Both women and men raised their hands to make their preferences known.

All of a sudden, we found ourselves with a completely different issue in dispute: Some of the women objected strongly to the men's participation in the voting process. It was really a philosophical issue: Although the men were submissive, their submission was role-playing—SM is, after all, a game. Many of us saw no reason to dismiss the men's opinions. It was a question of interpretation of roles, and while the women's attitudes towards the men were dominant in nature, we did acknowledge that this was role-playing and that, beneath their roles, the men were entitled to equal respect in this situation.

8

The Nuts and Bolts
of Whips and Chains*

SAFETY

Contrary to the demonology which portrays SM and its practitioners as dangerous psychopaths, safety is one of the most important—if not *the* most important—consideration for the vast majority of SM players. Media commonly portrays SM as dangerous and uncontrolled, with many news stories given SM "undertones" where none belong. These views reinforce the public beliefs about SM; they sell papers.

They are not true.

For example: Back in the early '80s in San Francisco, there was a major fire in an area of the city known to house some SM facilities. While battling this fire, a fire fighter reported the odor of burning meat. The press was quick to speculate that the fire had likely interrupted an SM scene and someone left tied to a bed had burned to death. The story ran until inspections of the burned buildings revealed no such human remains, and then it quietly disappeared from the press.

In 1986, a San Francisco criminal courtroom beheld the specter of a man being prosecuted (and convicted) of kidnap and rape, of keeping a woman as a "sex slave" against her will for seven years! His justification for his behavior: "She didn't mind. [She did]. We're just into bondage." [She wasn't.]

---

*This chapter was written and edited by JJ Madeson, and the use of the term *we* is meant to indicate that she is speaking as a member of the SM community.

The safe and responsible SM community cringes at such stories. The reputation of SM is bad enough without such extreme behavior being labeled—incorrectly—as SM. While understanding that such things can happen, the SM community strongly emphasizes that what separates these extremes from recreational SM activity is, once again, the all-important issue of consent.

We sadomasochists are playing sexual games, and it is obviously in everyone's best interests to play safely. Indeed, the few studies done within the SM community found a low rate of injuries among the participants, such results being attributed to a number of social arrangements in the subculture that specifically serve to reduce risk. For our own protection, then, myriad safety precautions have been built into both our social and sexual arenas.

Interaction often begins in "protected territories" such as leather bars or private locations that facilitate contact between SMers while screening out those whose interests are not as clearly focused. Such social networking—organized SM groups and special meeting places— enables us to "check out" potential partners with others who may know him (or her), discovering not only the individual's SM preferences but, most importantly, their reliability and sense of responsibility during play.

This last point may be the most important information of all and one that impacts most strongly on newcomers to the community. Until newcomers have patiently attended a number of social functions and made themselves known to more experienced SMers, they will have little opportunity to play with anyone other than their own partners. Because of the dangers of physical harm, disease, and the need for confidentiality, the SM community is slow to accept newcomers and few "old-timers" will play with an "unknown." This familiarization process can take many months, and the newcomers' first opportunities to play (with anyone other than their dates) will almost always take place at a party or group function where their play is both protected and monitored by the presence of others. Once the newcomer becomes better known and trusted, opportunities to participate fully in the community increase dramatically. The reasoning behind this process is clearly stated to interested newcomers so there are no surprises as they embark on their journey into the world of SM. The process, simply by its duration, acts to screen out those whose interest in SM is not sincere or sustained.

Another benefit of this social network is its ability to limit the activities and opportunities to play of those considered either unskilled or irresponsible in their play. There exists within the SM community an unspoken and unofficial "blacklist" (local for the most part, but wider, if necessary) where word of unacceptable behavior or unsafe practices can be passed informally through the community. Offenders will find themselves with few, if any, willing partners, not to mention a scarcity of invitations to play-oriented events. This is not punishment (well, I guess it is!); it is one of the ways our community protects itself.

In addition, two more facets of the SM subculture are designed to reduce risk: First, prior to actual SM play, the parameters of the play are routinely discussed and negotiated, potential activities set out, and limits set so the scene to come is fun, comfortable, and safe for all participants.

Secondly, interaction is controlled during the actual scenario by the open acknowledgment that anyone can withdraw at any time.

On a personal level, comments on the issue of safety make clear its importance in our play:

> I think an SM scene that is executed without guidelines and some talking and a little planning is ludicrous. It's a waste of time, and it's dangerous.

▼ ▼ ▼

> Isn't it obvious why we want to be safe? If I injure my partner, we won't be able to play until he's better, and that's no fun. So we're careful.

▼ ▼ ▼

> You can be really safe by knowing how not to damage people emotionally or physically. SM is only safe if you know what you're doing and that takes a certain amount of thinking, learning, practicing, and developing of sensitivity and skill. SM is very refined and complex sex play. It's not brute violence by any means, because brute violence doesn't work on people unless they're genuine martyrs, and we're not talking about martyrdom; we're talking about erotic fun.

▼ ▼ ▼

> Checking, communicating with your playmate, reading their body language, that's a part of it. Having talked it through beforehand, knowing—wanting to know—what's a turn-on and turn-off, that's what's important.

One of the organized SM groups that we will discuss later—a heterosexual male dominant/female submissive organization—originally accepted single men as members. Because the women in the group were sexually submissive, many of the single men seemed to feel it appropriate to adopt dominant roles with ANY of the women, bringing complaints from the women that group functions were taking on a "meat market" atmosphere that made them—and their dates—very uncomfortable. In response, single men are now welcome only if accompanied by a member. While such a policy has opened this and other groups to criticisms as being "couple oriented," the benefits of this practice seem to outweigh the criticism.

> Although my erotic fantasies and chosen SM role is submission, I am definitely unwilling to be submissive to others just because they may have dominant fantasies. On a social level, that's part of the game, and it's all in fun. On an intimate level, however, my submission is part of a negotiated agreement or relationship with a specific partner, and I really resent those who believe my submission relates to any dominant. That's not the idea at all.

At almost every SM group meeting, whether the program is discussion or demonstration, safety techniques and concerns play a primary part. For instance, bondage techniques are discussed with an eye towards the kind of rope to use, knots that will tie easily and, more importantly, release easily, all reinforced by the suggestion to keep a knife or scissors handy in case immediate release is necessary (more later).

If the topic is slapping, for example, a Top needs to know that he or she should have one hand under the submissive's jaw to support and steady the head, thus preventing neck or jaw injury; that fingers are better than the palm of the hand; and that the areas to be avoided are the nose, the eyes, the temples or even the ears (since a blow that cups the ear can burst an eardrum).

In a demonstration of whipping techniques, the safety issues would focus on a knowledge of anatomy aimed at awareness of where on the body such play is safest. The program might also cover what kinds of equipment will or will not leave marks, and the ways to control the level of pain inflicted.

> One of the things I find conspicuous about the people I have seen in these communities [SM] is the relatively high level of consciousness they exhibit about what they're doing and their willingness to investigate it farther.[1]

Additionally, those activities that are potentially dangerous or complicated (piercing, branding, the use of bull whips, etc.) are less frequent because the intense energies, concentration, and knowledge that go into these more complex activities are often reserved for special times. After all, SM's goal is a pleasurable erotic experience, and not one of us is interested in real harm, unintentional pain, or permanent damage.

DungeonMaster magazine, publishes many "how to" articles on various SM activities, and the publishers offer the following in each issue:

> In an attempt to offer guidelines, any article which discusses techniques or equipment will include the following classification system:
>
> G—General readership: Generally, a safe procedure for a novice using good sense and basic intelligence.
>
> TG—[Top]'s Guidance: An experienced [Top]'s guidance is recommended for at least some of the techniques included.
>
> R—Restricted: Novices should be closely supervised by an experienced [Top].
>
> X—Highly Restricted: Procedures should be attempted only by an experienced [Top].
>
> XXX—Avoid: Do not try this under any circumstances.[2]

SM practices, too, have undergone changes in the face of the current health dangers. For example, there is less sharing of toys, and most are taking better care of their equipment in terms of cleanliness. As a further example, many of us enjoy using latex dildoes in our play, and since these are almost always used vaginally or anally, they are potentially dangerous, and so condoms are used routinely over any such toys. We sadomasochists have made ourselves extremely knowledgeable on the subject of AIDS and health, and many—gay, bi, and straight—periodically take the AIDS antibody test. And almost all of us, even those with negative test results, have restricted or limited our play and/or choice of partners in some way. Indeed, we now are seeing a new challenge in our play: to eroticize the use of condoms and gloves and other necessary safety measures in a creative manner.

One SMer articulated the community's concern about AIDS this way:

> I don't know exactly why this is so, but it appears Californians have taken a more creative approach to this menace. The California SM

scene is, if anything, livelier and more vital than ever as we seek to adapt ourselves to the necessary precautions of our era with more innovative ways of expressing our erotic natures. Back east, everybody seems to have decided to stay home until the plague passes; they could be in for a long wait.

As someone who has been known to complain about the superficiality and trendiness of our part of the world, I have to give the California viewpoint its due in this particular situation. The openminded approach to innovative living for which the west is famous may just have found the specific challenge to which it is best suited.

SAFEWORDS

Aside from knowledge of anatomy and the skill we sadomasochists learn, the "safeword" or "key word" is the major mechanism by which SM practitioners guard against injury. A safeword is a word or phrase agreed upon prior to play which is used only if necessary by the submissive to signal the dominant that something is wrong. During any SM scene, the goal is pleasure, and occasionally one experiences sensations outside the intended SM activities that can divert or distract attention from the scene, and which, therefore, need to be brought to the attention of one's partner(s).

> Important note for dominants: Do not depend upon the submissive to say the safeword if she's reached her limits or is having a problem! As a dominant, you are responsible for knowing your submissive's condition at all times. A safeword is simply an additional safety valve.[3]

Most establish safewords during the communication and negotiation that precedes their play and it can be anything from "aardvark" to "mercy" to the use of the dominant's first name rather than "Master" or "Mistress," "Sir" or "Ma'am."

In recent years, a combination of two specific safewords, "red" and "yellow," (or sometimes even the word "safeword") has been almost universally accepted by the SM community. There are several advantages to such general agreement. First, common use of these same code words allows us to play with those we may not know well (at parties, for example) without confusion as to which partner prefers which word. In addition, the words themselves are easy to remember if and when they are needed.

In practice, the two words have separate meanings, allowing the submissive clearer communication to the dominant. "Yellow" is the first level and its use can mean a variety of things. This is the submissive's way of saying, for example, "I don't want to stop, but it's getting too intense. Please slow down or do something different" or "There's something I need to say; please ask me."

In a scenario involving bondage, for example, circulation to a hand or foot can be accidentally cut off by the tightness of the bonds themselves. While it is the dominant's responsibility to check for cold hands and feet (indicating diminished circulation), the submissive needs to bring the condition to the dominant's attention if he or she has not noticed it. A limb falling asleep, a chafing restraint or becoming uncomfortably cold can only serve to lessen the partners' pleasure for it interferes with concentration and the energy of the scene is thus diminished.

From the Bottom:

> I was in the middle of a wonderfully intense whipping scene. My hands were tied high above my head, and all my weight was resting on my high heels. The whips were secondary after a while—my feet were killing me! Had I simply kicked off my shoes, my feet would not have been able to touch the floor. So I said "yellow." He asked me what was up, and I explained the problem. He lowered my hands, removed my shoes, and we went back to what we were doing. It hadn't been enough of a problem to stop the scene completely—I didn't want it to stop at all—and so the safeword allowed us to adjust things so we could go on.

▼ ▼ ▼

> The pain was something I wanted, but being naked and cold was no fun. "Yellow" allowed me to say so. We turned up the heat and everything was back to "normal." I just didn't want to concentrate on anything but the energy between us, and the chill was getting in the way.

And from the Top:

> However dominant and in control of this game I am, it is still my responsibility—my obligation—to make sure the bottom is okay. It doesn't break the scene to quietly ask, "Are you okay?" We both ultimately bear the responsibility for any real trouble, but I think I have to be the one to ask often enough to free both of us from that worry.

The intense erotic energy and focus of an SM scene is usually enough to overcome most outside interference. Occasionally, though, sensations like those described above can become destructive to the energies at play. It may seem almost silly that people who enjoy whipping and other such activities would really be concerned about cold hands, but when concentration is broken, the fun stops. Without stopping the scene completely, the use of the yellow safeword allows the situation to be easily resolved. As with any safeword, it is used sparingly and not for insignificant reasons. A safeword is not used to "cry wolf."

The "red" safeword is more specific in its meaning: It means "Stop. Now." The specific reason for the "red" call becomes secondary until after the play has stopped completely and the participants can discuss what has happened.

Indeed, although play is almost never interrupted by those not directly involved, if a submissive at a party were to use "red" and the dominant did not stop the scene, someone else would step in and do so. Because the personal safety of the players is most important, adherence to the safeword system must be respected absolutely; it is a matter of trust and responsibility.

Having said all this about safewords, the reader may question why a submissive does not just say "Stop." The answer is that for the submissive to say "I need a break," or "Hey, you, I'm freezing!" violates the context of the scene and breaks both the fantasy and the mood of what is happening. This is, after all, role-playing, and despite the fact that the submissive has something to communicate, it needs to be done in a way that will keep the fantasy going. Unless, of course, it is a *true* emergency, where, safewords aside, whatever needs to be done or said to stop the play is acceptable, with no concern for subtlety or play roles.

Most sexually active people have found themselves in sexual situations saying "no, no, please don't" when what they really mean is "for God's sake, don't stop now!" (As one dominant remarked to a new submissive, "You say 'no' in such a 'yes' tone of voice!") Safewords allow the submissive to participate in the fantasy by saying "no, no" and meaning "yes, yes" without breaking the mood.

In that context, we remind you that SM is a *game*; it is role-playing, and what goes on while enacting a fantasy carries different connotations than it might in the "real world." The *fantasy* of SM and the activities during a play scene are clearly and openly differentiated here from true criminal acts such as rape where "no" means "no."

In fact, as part of the pre-play discussion/negotiation, the submissive is often told by the dominant: "You have the safeword. If you need it, use it. Other than that, I will pay no attention to any cries of 'no' or 'stop.'" The reader should understand that since these words clearly state the safeword rule, they also allow— and even encourage—appropriate contextual verbalization during a scene.

While most of us have established safewords with our specific play partners (or use the community standard), they are used infrequently.

> From my point of view as a submissive, the problem with safewords is that I hate to use them! When I'm playing, the last thing I want is for the scene to stop. If something is really wrong, of course, I'll use the safeword—but I'd put up with a great deal of discomfort before I'd force myself to call it quits with red. We do have them, of course, but the better I know my dominant and vice versa, the less I worry about needing them.

▾ ▾ ▾

> I want him to be deep into the play we are doing, and we can do that best if we can relax and not worry about outside things. We trust each other and while I do ask occasionally to make sure he's okay, he always has the safeword at his disposal. We both have the power to stop everything, and we trust each other enough to know that.

While safewords are not often used, they are usually implicit to the play in some way.

> Obviously, it's tough to say a safeword if your mouth is securely gagged or otherwise occupied. This quandary had never come up until I found myself at a party, hands bound over my head and a gag fixed tightly in my mouth. My dominant handed me a little rubber ball (anything small would have worked) and said quietly, "If you're in trouble, drop the ball." It was clever, subtle, and did not destroy the aesthetics or the mood of the scene. Now, when I'm dominant, I use that same technique with my submissives.

Additionally, those who play together often learn to "read" the body language of their partners and know exactly when the body is saying "too much" and when it is safe to continue.

> How do I know how tough I can be with her? Well, we've played together for years, and I read her. Her body responds to my whipping by its contortions, squirms, and moves. I can tell how intense or how far I can go from these little signs. It's almost involuntary on her part; it's her body reacting without benefit of the mind, so I know it's real.

▾ ▾ ▾

It's all part of the intensity and feedback. I'm giving him energy; he's giving energy back; and as I play with him, the energy flows back and forth between us. I feel and see his body movements—a sigh, a moan, a movement of his head, a twitch, ever so slight. This tells me where he is and how much further I can go. When I've reached his boundary of intensity, I take him one step further. He likes that.

▾ ▾ ▾

When it stops being pleasurable, then it's no longer fun, and we've reached our limits. I watch her body move, feel the flow of energy in both directions. Then, all of a sudden, there's a blockage or change in the energy and we can both feel it. That's a good time to take a break and replenish our energy so we can continue. It's subtle, though, that transfer of energy, but it's unmistakable.

▾ ▾ ▾

When I'm bottoming [being submissive], the heavier and more intense the scene becomes, the quieter I become, moving sometimes into an almost trancelike state. If I play with someone I don't know very well, this kind of information needs to be discussed in advance. Otherwise, there we are in the middle of a heavy scene, I get quiet and still and my dominant thinks I'm catatonic when what I really am is turned on. The dominant needs to know this up front so there is no misinterpretation of signals.

LIMITS

In SM play, "limits" are activities that one prefers not to or will not do— personal boundaries—whether due to personal feelings, negative past experiences or lack of practice. Such limits might include a low pain threshold, a fear of needles, or a dislike of tight bondage. Any physical limitations that could affect play, such as a sore arm, a tender breast, etc., falls into this category as well, and it is the submissive's responsibility to inform the dominant of such things ahead of time as much as it is the responsibility of the dominant to ask. Limits are most often set during pre-play discussion, and respect for a partner's limits is the foundation of the trust between the players.

When I was first getting into SM, I spent a lot of time talking with a female confidante who was a bit more experienced. We would discuss all sorts of activities that we had or had not tried, and often I found myself saying, "Oh, I'd never do that." Her response was always, "Talk to me in six months, and never say never." She was almost always right. Six months later, I'd be doing and loving just what I'd said I wouldn't do, and finding new limits in other things about which I'd be saying, "Oh, I'd never do that."

▼ ▼ ▼

How far can we take our pleasures? As long as it's pleasurable for both of us, we keep exploring and expanding. Limits are set so we have a framework in which to work and the limits are often expected to be expanded. Limits are based on when it stops being fun. We're not here to see if I can beat him black and blue, or raw and bloody. That's not the purpose at all. The purpose is to give and receive pleasure. So our limits are when we stop doing that.

Change is integral to sexual growth and so while it is necessary to discuss and set limits, they are rarely written in stone. Time, experience, and practice can promote change, and limits can be pushed and expanded with sensitive exploration.

Pushing or stretching limits describes erotic encounters in which a dominant presses the submissive to accept a greater level of stimulation [or a different kind of stimulation] than the submissive originally expected.[4]

▼ ▼ ▼

Pushing limits is harder than it might seem. Dignity drops by the wayside when I'm pushed; only instinct exists and I have had to learn that my instinctual self—my animal self—is okay, too, and can be trusted.

▼ ▼ ▼

What does "pushing limits" mean to me? As a submissive, it means I want a Top who won't listen when I kick and scream, but will still pay close attention. The amount of pain that somebody can handle is not really fixed, and there are ways to increase it. A limit is a point that's always changing.

▼ ▼ ▼

Tops learn about their submissives and play accordingly. The SM activity ideally reflects both partners' fantasies. The intensity must be enough to eroticize the bottom's limits, though too much can be destructive and a turn-off. It's a fine line.

A simple example: The submissive expresses a dislike of being slapped. As play progresses, the dominant may lightly tap or caress the submissive's face with a hand, sensitive to the response. If it is negative, the activity will most likely be abandoned and play will move on to something else. If, however, the response seems positive, the dominant may push further, perhaps with a harder tap of a hand on the face, until—and if—a negative response is forthcoming. The submissive, at the end of this "experiment," may well say, "Wow. I sure didn't think I'd like that, but it was really hot!"

During the course of an SM scene, for example, a dominant may use the technique of verbal humiliation by saying to the submissive, "You are so open and vulnerable. You'd let anybody do anything to you, wouldn't you? What a slut." Humiliation is created here since the submissive knows that there is a part of his or her personality about which the statement (or other similar ones) is true, but is embarrassed that someone would notice or recognize that part and point it out. That embarrassment—the recognition of the intimacy and vulnerability—is the root of the eroticism of humiliation. On the other hand, if such expressions were not meant as erotic, they would never find their way into SM play at all.

The truth, however—and the fact that makes it role-playing—is that the submissive knows the dominant is implying neither a lack of respect nor a denigration of the submissive's character since the partners' equality in the relationship is, hopefully, well-established.

Using the dominant's intimate knowledge about and control of the submissive, and playing with them in an SM scene, can be a safe way to act out those parts of the submissive's personality that are uncomfortable. The issue once again is trust; were this same language or import to be used by someone the submissive did not know or in a context that is not erotic, it would indeed be too real and insulting. SM play is an opportunity to bring out the hidden, secret parts of a personality, put them in perspective by exaggerating them without the consequential long-term loss of self-esteem that would exist were the statements malicious.

Fortunately, most of us are responsible and rarely "hit below the belt." That means there are few dominants who would, as a tool to create a humiliation trip for the submissive, use facts or feelings that are too sensitive. In other words, if I am overweight and worried about it, my dominant would be betraying my trust by using that information in order to humiliate me. Again, this is a matter of trust, of how well the players know each other, and the sense of responsibility and caring that the partners have for each other. SM is a separate world from "out there"—getting away from the world is one of the main reasons for

SM play at all—and some things that are too "real world" can break the fantasy mood and destroy the scene, if not the relationship. Since the goal is fun, that kind of injury would be unfair, nonconsensual and unsuccessful.

It is possible that limits are determined as much by the evolving fantasy as they are by physiological considerations such as pain thresholds. It is also true that an individual's limits can vary with the degree of intimacy. Thus, in those situations where intimacy is greatest, such as interaction with a lover who knows one's needs, limits tend to be more loosely defined, whereas in scenarios with new partners, they are more closely controlled. Frequent interaction lessens the need for specific guidelines, not only because of increasing familiarity but because of the development of trust.

While growth and change motivate most efforts to push limits, there are some instances where limits are pushed to prove the depth of one's submission or simply because the dominant wants it.

> The minute it became too heavy, I just started loving her more, and there was a point when limits almost disappeared for me, where I just gave up all resistance completely. I suppose a Top could seriously hurt somebody in that space where the bottom would say, "Sure, why not?" because they've given up all responsibility. But this is why it's important for us to be aware, to trust each other and to be really skilled, to really know and understand our partners.

▾ ▾ ▾

You push and you push and
it hurts and it hurts and
I strain towards a goal . . .
And the dawn finally breaks
and the sun also rises,

. . . and . . . I'm there.

I look in your eyes
as you push me and push me
and push me,
and it hurts and it hurts . . .

. . . until . . . I'm there.

And the dam breaks
and the sun also rises

And my mind has been reduced
to one word,
to one single thought:

Yes. To Anything.

And only then am I free.

The exploration of limits is not without its own limits. While some
may occasionally find their limits pushed further than they want, few
exhibit a "do it at all costs" attitude. Safety and reason predominate,
even in fantasy. The usual result of these experiences is a sore body
and recognition that a miscalculation was made, which, in the long run,
serves to strengthen and clarify communication between the partners.

Like submissives, dominants, too, have limits. The difference here,
though, is that since the dominant is in control, anything the dominant
does not want to do simply is not done. But the concept is important,
and responsible dominants are willing to acknowledge their own limits.

> I was whipping him very hard and he was begging me for more. It
> was too much for me, even if it wasn't for him, so I slowed it down
> a bit. My prerogative; I'm in charge!

> ▾ ▾ ▾

> Anyone who calls him or herself a dominant who isn't willing to
> look back at something and say "I screwed up" doesn't deserve the
> title and is probably not a very good top. There's humility in domi-
> nance; there has to be. One of the biggest secrets to being a good Top
> is knowing that you are not infallible and that you can screw up.
> That's very important when you take on the responsibility of this
> person who is giving himself to you.

> ▾ ▾ ▾

> My submissive had been "borrowed"—with my permission,
> obviously—by another dominant during a party. I was socializing at
> the time and after a while, I wandered back into the playroom to
> watch the fun and keep an eye on my "property." He was being
> whipped with a small bull whip by the dominant to whom I had lent
> him. Although he is a "heavy" submissive and can take a lot of pain,
> I could tell he was being pushed. He seemed okay, but as I watched,
> I realized that what was going on was too heavy for ME! I couldn't
> handle the intensity and the level of pain I knew was being inflicted.
> MY limits had been passed. He could probably handle it, but I couldn't
> and he was mine. So, for about the second time in my SM life, I

exercised my prerogative as his Master and stopped the scene. It was done tactfully and there were no hard feelings. He had no way of knowing why I'd chosen that time to interrupt, but I simply thanked the "borrower" on his behalf for an intense experience and said that I wanted my property back.

I pondered the experience a while later and decided that, although it had been difficult, I had done the right thing. I certainly had the right to call a halt—after all, I'm the dominant! My submissive does what I say. That I had the right to do what I did was never an issue for either of us, but I did have to deal with feelings about my own limits and allow myself to have them.

There are sometimes activities that are true limits, ones that cannot be pushed.

My lover and I play very intensely and one of the things we used to play with was [sterile surgical] needles [for temporary piercing]. My lover is a surgeon so he certainly knows what he is doing, but several times in a row when we were playing with needles, I got frightened— too frightened—and the scene was ruined because I simply couldn't handle what was happening. The fear was paralyzing. Finally, we talked about it and decided—as much as I hate saying *no* to anything—that needles were a real limit for me, one we would not push.

Fear is fun to play with, but terror is not, and in this case, the terror I felt was in no way erotic and was simply not worth the price for either of us. So, we agreed that at least for a while—a LONG while—needles were out. This agreement makes going into a scene easier for me; at least I know what's NOT going to happen, and so I can relax and concentrate on the things that DO. Our play is as intense and fun as ever, and I'm much more relaxed. I enjoy the fantasy of fear but terror is too much.

Another point that needs to be made here is that while there are certainly activities and concepts that have unbreachable limits, they are nonetheless erotic and exciting on a fantasy level—to read about, fantasize about, talk about or even threaten. It must be clear, though, that these are but fantasies. This kind of teasing or threatening behavior fall into the area of psychological pain and will be discussed in chapter 11.

TOYS

In another throwback reference to childhood games, we call anything that contributes to the mood and the atmosphere of SM play a toy!

By this definition, toys include lighting, costuming, and even music. Usually, though, toys are specific pieces of SM equipment, and they come in incredible varieties—from the handmade whip costing $250 to a simple spatula that most of us have in our kitchens. An experienced dominant once said that "if you can't create a complete scene from what's in the kitchen, you're not really into SM!"

Since SM (and most vanilla sexual activity) is so dependent upon imagination, SM scenes can be played with no toys at all, but for those whose requirements include a great many custom-made toys, SM as a sexual lifestyle can be very expensive. On the other hand, the toy collection is the greatest opportunity to experiment with one's own sense of handiness and creativity.

Leather is the traditional "material of choice" for most SM toys because it is easily available and leather toys tend to last a long time— a great advantage considering the expense of such items. Leather (like latex or rubber) is the object of many fetishists, usually because of its strength, color, texture, and, in some cases, smell. Feathers, fur, and suede (there are even whips made of suede) are also widely used, as SM is basically a sensual experience.

Toys are of an infinite variety. Anything from pocket combs to sandpaper (when pulled over sensitive skin, either can be both erotic and somewhat painful, although sandpaper can easily cause bleeding), from restraints to the most expensive dungeon setups including cages, medical exam tables, racks, and bondage crosses, can be used. Some people have toy collections worth thousands of dollars; others have become handy at making equipment themselves, thereby relieving some of the financial costs of such a lifestyle; others have virtually no equipment at all.

The proper and safe use of toys is, without question, the most important component of the physical aspects of SM play. Whether we are using hands to spank or a $300 custom-made flogger, a certain knowledge of anatomy is imperative in the safe "art" of SM play, and such knowledge is gained through reading, informational and educational programs, watching and talking to others, learning and practicing. Additionally, almost all elements of SM safety are matters of simple common sense.

The following is a quick guideline to safety issues with some of the most common SM toys. This is by no means a complete list of toys nor are the safety measures discussed the only considerations with these toys.

Whips, Straps, Crops, and Canes

It is necessary to know, for example, that one should never use any toy to strike the head, neck, or spine, and to avoid joints and ligaments such as knees, ankles, wrists, or elbows. One must know that the kidneys are just above the buttocks and so that area has little anatomical protection, meaning injury could result should these areas be struck.

Almost any toy used for striking the buttocks, for instance, is far safer than when used anywhere else, simply because of the padding the body provides in that area. But here again, it is necessary to remember that if someone is bending over, the body's own layers of protection shift and bone comes closer to the skin without as much padding.

When using a whip, however, even on the buttocks, one needs to know that if the tips of the lashes reach around and strike the front or side of the body (e.g., the hip bone or the abdomen), a "no-no" called "wrapping," the pain created is far greater than intended. The same is true whether you are targeting the buttocks or the back and, in some cases, even the breasts. Wrapping is usually a sign of either a missed stroke or a novice Top, and every submissive will do whatever is necessary to register a complaint about such technique.

A Top needs to know that when a flogger (whip) is used, the greatest force is present at the tips of the lashes (strands) and where the tips land will be the most painful and intense area; one wants to know that the longer the lashes, the harder the whip is to control; the softer the lashes, the harder it can be safely used; and the more lashes on the whip, the less intense will be its impact.

A Top should know that a whip of almost any kind lands with a "thud" or a "thwack" whereas a hand, a paddle, a crop or a cane makes a very stingy impact, which is in some ways more painful. Paddles, crops and canes, however, are easier to aim than a flogger and the pain caused is more concentrated.

> I've always believed that using any toy like whips, paddles, or canes, there is some valid comparison to be made with a tennis player, believe it or not! When a tennis player hits a ball exactly right, the ball's position on the racket makes a very specific sound. The same is true in SM. When the whip lands just the way it is supposed to, the sound it makes is solid. If it's off target a little, you can tell from the sound.

When Tops pick up and use a toy, they are expected to know exactly how that toy is properly used, what it *feels* like on the body and the kind of bruises, if any, it will cause. They should have tried the toy on themselves (usually on a hand, arm, buttocks, or thigh) in order to understand its use and impact. If the Top is a switch, he or she may well have experienced the toy from the other end, so to speak. A Top who has no idea what a toy feels like to the submissive is being irresponsible and unsafe.

When the genitals are involved in SM play, the safety issues and kind of toys that can be used are somewhat different from those used on the rest of the body. Common sense will obviously need to be used along with whatever toys one feels are appropriate. That sense tells us that the genital areas are very, very sensitive, and that the kinds of blows one can use to the buttocks cannot be used on or near the genitals. Damage can be caused much more easily to male genitalia since the testicles and penis are outside the body, easier to reach, and tend to have thinner skin. Since most genitalia are protected by a significant amount of hair, those men or women who have removed pubic hair need to be treated somewhat more tenderly in those areas.

All of these and other kinds of things need to be considered when choosing any toy for use in the genital and/or breast areas. Most common here are small whips or softer paddles, and almost every kind of clamp can be used in these areas as well. One should be aware, however, that the duration of any play directly involving the genitals or breasts needs to be much shorter. Where you might be able to flog someone's buttocks for an hour or more without stopping (except to tend to your sore arm!), the same is not true with the genital and breast areas.

Clips and Clamps

The least expensive and most common items used as clamps in SM play are either rubber bands or the simple clothespin, and here again, the creative possibilities are endless. I have seen some great toys made out of popsicle sticks and rubber bands! Considerations here are that clothespins are often tighter and more painful than desired, and often need to be partially sprung before use, not to mention the necessity for making sure the wood itself is smooth and will not cause splinters.

Clamps can be used anywhere on the body but their most common use is on breasts, nipples, and genitals. Clamps must be used carefully, keeping in mind that the less skin caught in the clamp, the more pain the process will produce.

Additionally, whereas the placement and application of the clamp(s) will be somewhat painful, their removal will cause even more intense pain as the numbed area and nerve endings are suddenly filled with the onrush of returning blood. This pain can be minimized (should one want to do so) by slow removal. No clamps should be left on for more than twenty to thirty minutes at the risk of more permanent damage, and clamps on more sensitive areas such as labial lips, nipples, or male genitalia should be either moved or removed every few minutes.

> When someone puts clamps on me, it hurts a lot when they go on; then the area kind of goes numb if left alone. But I know the whole time I'm wearing them that it'll hurt like hell when they come off (more so the longer they've been on), and I'd be hard-pressed to decide whether to experience that pain now or later (not that it's my decision). It's kind of a double-bind, I think!

▼ ▼ ▼

> A form of painless throbbing, a numbness, replaces the previous and raw state of pain. And with this transformation, a slowly creeping wave of euphoria falls into place.[5]

Occasionally, clamps with uncovered alligator tips can be used, although more often the tips will be covered with plastic, rubber, or vinyl caps, a safer and more comfortable (!) style. Further, any clamps that have smooth tips are far easier to clean and therefore safer to use.

Dildoes and Other Insertibles

Regardless of whether the object you wish to insert is a finger, a hand, a vibrator, a banana, or a dildoe and where that insertion is to be (vagina or anus), safety is probably more an important consideration here than anywhere else. First of all, invasion into the human body is a delicate operation and the condition of one's insides are for the most part unknown, so any internal activity should be gentle rather than forceful. Secondly, it is in this kind of play more than any other that health is a concern, most specifically AIDS. Dildoes and other similar toys can be made of rubber or plastic with the latter being less absorbent of germs and therefore, again, safer.

When it comes to insertion play, however, including anal or vaginal sex, it can be made safer with the knowledge that the AIDS virus seems unable to penetrate latex, and latex is available in both condoms and gloves. Any lubricant to be used (and some should be) should be water-based rather than oil-based (for cleaning purposes and because oil-based products can cause breaks in latex) and should specifically contain non-oxynol 9, a chemical which kills the AIDS virus. A good part of anyone's "sex budget" is well spent on the highest quality products available.

One should never insert anything into the anus or the vagina that is fragile, breakable, overly large or that is open at the internal end, as such a toy can create a vacuum that could make removal a task only for a physician. Also, anything used during anal play should be shaped such that it cannot be inserted completely, a circumstance which would also require a physician's help to remove it.

After using a dildoe for either vaginal or anal play, it must be thoroughly cleaned with soap, water, and/or bleach, and if the dildoe does not belong to the person it is being used on, it should first be covered with one or two strong condoms and plenty of water-soluble lubricant.

Dildoes should be used gently and slowly, and it should be kept in mind that those which can be bent usually have a wire inside that holds the shape firm. If used in too rough a manner, it is possible for the wire to poke through and do serious internal damage.

Sharps

The use of needles and/or knives is considered an extreme SM activity otherwise known as "edge play." Use of such instruments must be done with the same extraordinary care expected of any medical practitioner, including the wearing of sterile gloves, the use of only sterile instruments, the cleaning of the skin before and after with Betadine or alcohol (assuming you have first asked about allergies), and most importantly, complete knowledge and experience of what you are doing.

Needles can be used in SM play for temporary or permanent piercing and should always be inserted parallel to the surface of the skin in an enter/exit manner rather than straight down into the skin. Most often, a cork is positioned at the point where the needle exits to absorb the sharp end and prevent the piercer from getting stuck with a blood-coated needle. When removed, needles should be capped and permanently discarded in a way that makes sure they are inaccessible.

Another variation for sharps play is the neurological pinwheel that is, unlike a needle, a reusable instrument, necessitating highly specific cleaning before and after use, especially if it causes bleeding.

Dear Columnist: Last weekend our condominium neighbors interrupted a great session between my lover and me. She was yelling so loudly while getting spanked that they thought some woman was in real danger, so they got the manager to barge in with his master key, right in the middle of everything! What on earth should we do now?

A. Try to orchestrate your life so your neighbors will think that you're just another noisy, quarrelsome couple. If you do get a surprise interruption, be ready with the all-purpose-natural-health-care explanation: clamps can be passed off as "acupressure equipment," corsets and collars can plausibly be "chakra sleeves," and most bondage can be made to appear as "compressing the energy channels."

Finally, be prepared for anything by attending my upcoming adult-education class, "How to Turn SM Toys into Ordinary Household Objects." You'll learn how to handle home emergencies by instantly turning a whip into a braided belt from L. L. Bean, a cat-o'-nine tails into a designer dustmop from Crate & Barrel, and a pair of handcuffs into a set of embroidery hoops from Payless Drugs![6]

Many of the toys used in SM have more of a "show" value than a "use" value. For example, some paddles are designed to create a great deal of noise, but hurt very little; other toys do not make much noise, but do hurt more. Additionally, some toys will leave marks where others will not, an option that depends on the preferences and experience of the players.

Dear Columnist: I'm a pain-craving woman who loves getting flogged, paddled, and whipped to shreds. I also have sensitive skin that bruises easily, so I usually have marks on my body. I'd like to take aerobic dance and exercise classes at my health club, but I'm not yet ready to tell the other women in the locker room how I got my lovely welts. What should I say if they ask me about my marks?

A. The best approach is fake honesty. When they ask, answer in a simple, earnest voice, "Well, I do S&M," but with the facial expression and vocal tone as if you were lying. The rest of the conversation will probably go like this: "Yeah, right!" "No, I really do that." "Haw, haw. Sure." "No, listen, I got whipped and tormented last night." "Oh bullshit. How'd it really happen?"[7]

There is an art to SM; the techniques are learned and practiced, modified, and practiced some more. Only then are they put into use. Indeed, for safety's sake, the acknowledged premise and practice is: "When in doubt, don't."

BONDAGE

Almost any SM or sexual activity can be intensified and eroticized by the use of bondage. As we saw in "Love Letters" in the introduction to this book, bondage can be a highly spiritual experience in that its physical and psychological effects can be overwhelming.

> Here is an image of human strength and human fragility. The inescap-able frailty of the human condition, as a man who is bound and stilled as any of us can be at any moment. This bound body speaks ironically of peace and freedom.
>   For the top sees his own frailty intrinsically tied to his own strength. The strength of his own creation, a human sculpture built of another's frailty and conviction; the strength of a human body frozen in its glory.[x]

Bondage is the ultimate manifestation of the fantasy of helplessness, and this is where the fantasy becomes reality because, in bondage, movement is restricted, if not impossible.

Bondage can be short-term (for a few minutes) or long-term (up to a few hours or even overnight), and the "rope work" itself can be simple or as complicated as a spider's web.

> When she's binding me, even if I'm wearing a blindfold, I feel the ropes go into place in and around my body, and I can see in my mind the picture of what she is creating. It feels as beautiful as it looks. Or is it that it looks as beautiful as it feels?!

▾   ▾   ▾

> Come on, admit it. There is something about the idea of someone in bondage that is highly erotic, isn't there? Even women feel it, so it's not just a "guy thing." What words come to mind? Helplessness. Powerlessness. Tension. Sex. Lust. Heat.

There are safety considerations associated with the use of restraints or rope bondage just as there are such considerations with any other type of SM experience.

The first consideration is breathing. More oxygen is needed during sexual excitement, most often because breathing becomes far more rapid, and while no restraint should ever be used around the neck, even tight bonds on chest or stomach can make breathing more difficult. Additionally, because of this consideration, one firm rule of bondage is that one who is bound is never left alone. Period.

The second consideration is the tightness of the restraints, an issue because of the possibility of cutting off circulation to any area of the body. A cold hand or foot in an otherwise warm room is an indication of such a condition, fixed simply by loosening the bonds; tingly, "going to sleep" sensations in a hand or foot or any other body part is another indication of the same thing. This entire issue can be resolved during the initial placement of the restraint by making sure that at least one finger can fit between the rope and your partner's skin.

The next most significant safety consideration here is release, which is important both when the dominant partner wants to remove the restraints and move on or in the event an emergency release is necessary. There are two safety precautions here: First, keep a sharp scissors or knife handy for instant release; and secondly, soft nylon rope or fur-padded restraints are both easier to release or untie and much more comfortable to the "bondee."

If one is into bondage, relatively inexpensive magician's rope is often the bond of choice because this kind of rope is soft, smooth, and slick, allowing for comfort as well as quick and easy release. Nylon rope or clothesline is the next best choice, but because of its unyielding rigidity, it needs to be washed several times before use to soften it. The softer the better to avoid rope burns and just to make it comfortable. ("I love pain but I DON'T like being uncomfortable!")

As we have mentioned before, the comfort of the submissive in SM play is an important consideration. Whatever physical sensations the dominant wishes the submissive partner to feel should be achieved in such a way that the scene is free from unintentional pain or sensation, which we call "bad pain." The specific intent of bondage is to focus attention *only* on the physical and/or psychological sensations the dominant wants the submissive to feel, and outside or unplanned influences can only be disruptive.

Bondage, as with every other SM activity, lends itself to the challenge of the imagination. Here, not only are rope and special restraints available for use, but so is ribbon, wire, string, leather straps and belts, chains, and even—are you ready for this?—plastic wrap. Really. Once again, we point out the obvious: No bondage equipment or techniques should ever be used in any way so as to restrict breathing. This is the dominant's ultimate responsibility and the submissive's ultimate show of trust.

"Pain Bondage" is a variation in which some pain-causing mechanism such as nipple clamps or genital clamps (or both) are attached directly from the skin to an immovable object that forms the other end of such bondage (such as a wall, a post, the ceiling) by means of chains or ropes. In other words, *whatever* movement the bottom tries to make during this kind of bondage (sometimes even just breathing), will cause pain and will directly effect the tautness and the pinch of these clamps, causing an increase in pain. In such a technique, even the usual bondage tools such as rope or leather restraints are not even necessary.

> The tighter those clamps are, the less I am able to move, and any movement I do make causes further pain. I am never allowed to forget that fact. It's an exciting experience. Very intense. Very calming.

A second bondage technique is invisible (or psychological) bondage in which the submissive's movement is restricted, at the clear command of the Top, only by his or her own will power.

> We play this game he loves; it's called the "You'd Better Not Move" game. (I actually love it, but I'll be damned if I'll tell him that!) When he stretches my arms and legs out and says that if I move anything, I will be punished, I believe him. I know that the punishment will be worse than whatever he intends to do anyway, and for me, the stronger the demand, the more attention I will focus on not moving. Not only because of the threat that hangs over my head but because this is what he demands of me, and I will do anything I can to obey him.

▼   ▼   ▼

> The hardest thing about invisible bondage is the challenge it presents, since for the duration of it, he will also be enduring some sort of play that may well be painful and keeping still will be that much harder.

▼   ▼   ▼

> When he quietly whispers, "Good girl," I know I have done well, enduring what he asked of me. I am proud of myself and he is proud of me. I have successfully handled a difficult challenge; I did it. If I can do this, I can do anything. I will take that knowledge with me in the next few days or weeks and will be stronger for it.

Sensory deprivation and sensory overload are two other forms of bondage controlling sensory input, thus directing concentration only along the specific paths the dominant chooses to follow.

Deprivation is a restriction of some very basic physical capabilities and can include such devices as a blindfold to cut off sight, gags to cut off verbal response, earplugs to cut the sound input, or even full-head hoods to restrict any or all of the above senses at the same time.

In the blackness of the blindfold, your whole world becomes what he makes of it. Every sensation is magnified, nerve-ends and imagination replacing vision.[9]

▼ ▼ ▼

The more senses, other than physical touch, that I can cut off on her body, the more intense are the sensations she *can* feel. I am well aware of that, and I also know that under these circumstances, even the lightest, most tender caress feels like a live wire touched to her skin.

▼ ▼ ▼

In the kind of play my husband and I like to do, I rarely use a gag on him because the sounds he makes—the groans, the whimpers, the "yes, please's" and the "no, please don't's," even the tears—really turn me on. Him, too, if the truth be told.

▼ ▼ ▼

It frightens me not to be able to hear because if I'm blindfolded, my *only* sensory input (not to mention hints of what's to come) is aural before it's physical. When I don't know what's about to happen, the anticipation and fear is highly increased. It's like the difference between knowing specifically what the dentist is going to do, where you can attempt to prepare yourself and control your fear, and not knowing exactly what is to be done, where anticipation itself comes into play. (The dentist analogy is not a great one, I know, but it's what came to mind!)

Sensory overload seems a self-explanatory term, but here are a few examples:

Sometimes I turn the music up really loud, blindfold him, cover him with clamps and whip him. It sort of blows his mind and he ends up just about screaming, not because it hurts that much, but because he doesn't know exactly what to concentrate on first, last, or next. It makes me crazy with lust because I can do a little of everything and drive him nuts with confusion and sensation.

▼ ▼ ▼

Last night, he blindfolded me, tied my hands behind my back and pushed me first into a cold shower and then into a wonderful warm one. I was so overwhelmed not knowing what he could possibly think of next, I just started to laugh. There was nothing else I could do; it was instinctual. He joined me in that laughter, and after a few minutes, we hugged in the shower (the warm one), dried ourselves off and went on from there. What an experience!

FANTASY

As has been well documented by the popularity of the numerous books on the subject of sexual fantasy (Nancy Friday's *Men in Love, Secret Garden* or *Forbidden Flowers*), almost all of us at some time or another in our lives have fantasies. Whether we remember them or not, whether we "approve" of their content or not, everyone has them.

We sadomasochists are no different, although I will admit that our fantasies are often more detailed than many, if only because we have not only freely acknowledged them to ourselves and to others in our world, but have sometimes gone so far as to act them out in SM play.

> SM shows us how to turn even our "worst" fantasies into pleasure for both of us so we know that what is inside us is okay.

Indeed, though we often believe our fantasies and their mere existence seems "crazy" to those outside SM looking in, even the mainstream press has done articles such as the one below:

> How is your fantasy life? Is it OK for you to fantasize? If not, you are probably cheating yourself out of a very important human experience.
>
> And why are fantasies so important? Current research suggests that your fantasy life can help with personal adjustment and overcoming stress. In fact, improving your fantasy life could be a key factor to improving your mental and physical health. . . . Appreciating your fantasy life is a healthy sign; it doesn't mean you're crazy.
>
> Most of our fantasies are about sex, travel, wealth, food, or fame. A lot of our fantasy material comes from television, movies, advertisements, books, magazines, and, of course, conversations and personal encounters. A well-developed fantasy can result in a pleasurable state of physical and mental relaxation.
>
> A friend recently said to me, "I've got some fantasies you wouldn't believe!" In many ways, it's healthy to believe our fantasies have our own personal stamp of creation. However, many of our fantasies are quite common. We all share the same culture, the same images and experiences.
>
> We needn't be embarrassed about our fantasies. In fact, talking about them with someone we trust can be helpful. We may discover that we are not so alone, bizarre and sick.
>
> It's too bad that so many adults have lost touch with their fantasy life. Fantasizing should be a lifelong joy.[10]

Fantasies during sexual play are common for both men and women, and SM-style lovemaking can fulfill some of those fantasies.

"Fantasies are hungrier than bodies,"[11] meaning that our fantasies can often be more extreme than anything we'd ever want to experience in reality. Most of us are also in agreement with the idea that fantasy is, by definition, consensual; if you don't like what you're fantasizing, you have total power to change the scene.

As noted above, fantasies often exceed the reality of what we would truly like to experience.

Among the fantasies that I share with my lover are those that scare even me with their brutality or what they seem to say about me. Some of them actually embarrass me to tears, but if I choose to share them, he always seems to understand. Most of the time, though, I'm really clear that I'm just fantasizing out loud.

▼　▼　▼

Sometimes we arrange a time to act out a specific fantasy. I wonder ahead of time if I'll survive the experience of sharing *that* much intimacy, not to mention the shame that some of my fantasies bring me. Then, later that night, just before I drift off to sleep, new fantasies creep in, fantasies even MORE intimate and embarrassing.

At first I was disappointed by this. After all, we'd just spent a lot of time and effort making a fantasy come true. I'd accepted with difficulty that they were part of me and that it was okay. And now, my imagination seemed to be going EVEN farther. I understand now that my mind will always create fantasies that go farther than I am able, and I guess I'm just lucky to have such a vivid imagination!

Fantasies are natural and normal products of the imagination. Whether the fantasy is that of a helpless maiden held captive by pirates, the hunter found by primitive tribesmen and prepared as their next meal, the victim of a fictional Inquisition or just making love to Tom Selleck, all of these (well, almost all!) and more can be played out safely:

At first, I didn't understand fantasies, probably because I was never in touch with very many of my own, and I was hurt that he fantasized so much. I figured if we were playing and he were fantasizing about someone or something else, I must be doing something wrong or he was bored.

Later I learned that most often he was taking what was actually happening and adding a "story line" to it. I was not being ignored at all. What we were doing was like a starting point, and whatever we did was imaginatively put right into his fantasy. Now, I know how to facilitate and guide the fantasy so that it becomes a part of what we're doing rather than a separate event.

Nonconsensuality lies behind many sexual fantasies, including the oft-mentioned rape fantasies. True rape is a nonconsensual act while a rape *fantasy* is a consensual "sex game," negotiated ahead of time by all participants, who have either scripted the entire scenario in advance, discussed the activities that are desired and/or permissible, or at least delineated the physical and/or psychological limits that may be explored. In a rape fantasy, you can change it, stop it, or modify it; an actual rape has no such control.

We would strongly emphasize here that while it may be true that fantasies about being raped can, for many women, be very erotic, true rape is not desired. Rape is an aggressive, violent act; SM activities are sexual in nature. Rape is not consensual; SM is. These facts clearly separate the reality of rape from the fantasy, and once this concept is understood, the myth that equates SM with rape can be dispelled.

> I was raped as a teenager and have never forgotten the horrible reality of the experience. It took lots of therapy and hard work, but now, many years later, when my partner and I act out a rape fantasy, I do find myself turned on by the *sexuality* of the fantasy without any confusion at all as to the difference between my past experience and the sexual games we play now.

SM fantasy play can allow experience of the rough sexuality and powerlessness that are the main components of the eroticism of rape, and consensually playing out this or any other nonconsensual fantasy can be fun and safe by acknowledging that we have chosen our partner, the time, and the place, and that all details have been planned (sometimes even scripted) in advance.

Whether the subject matter of the fantasy is consensual or nonconsensual, the variety is endless. Anything from Westerns, prison escape, futuristic/alien scenes, slinky 1930s Bonnie and Clyde scenarios, military officer/enlisted man, professional environment (corporate bosses administering corporal punishment) to Catholic school caning stories—all can be explored creatively and safely by experienced sadomasochists.

DRUGS AND ALCOHOL

Serious abuse of drugs and alcohol in the SM community is rare, although in the past few years, 12-Step groups have been formed specifically to support "leatherfolk" who need to renew their commitment to "safe and sane" sadomasochism and/or staying "clean and sober."

Moderate use of marijuana, beer, or wine seems to be the choice for most who use these substances, and while one must take note of drugs' potential numbing effects on the workings of the mind and even on pain sensors, limited use of some drugs can lower the inhibitions that are sometimes barriers to SM play.

Drugs and alcohol are considerations in the SM community due to their potential effect on SM play, and the two issues of greatest importance here are control and performance. Obviously, someone high on drugs or alcohol is neither trustworthy nor safe, and as we have seen, trust and safety are the key components of successful SM play.

Reflecting the SM community's emphasis on safety is a flyer for newcomers that handled the issue this way:

> Alcohol and other drugs are okay, but *don't* overdo it! People who are wiped on drugs are a drag and a drain on the hot energy that makes a good party work. People who don't take responsibility for themselves don't get invited back!

And again:

> BOOZE AND DRUGS: Both are allowed but moderation is advised. *Never use them as a substitute for true relaxation.* We all know there are better ways to overcome your inhibitions.

Drug use often differs between submissives and dominants. Although the use of drugs and alcohol always needs to be carefully monitored when doing SM, the submissive generally needs somewhat less control over the situation than does the dominant (another example of the need for trust). The use of drugs or alcohol is usually regulated accordingly. One woman, for example, enjoys marijuana but will not use any if she is being dominant; she needs to be fully in control and able to react appropriately. But when she is submissive and has her dominant's permission, she does use it. Even for the submissive, though, drugs can shorten reaction time should a safeword be needed or an emergency occur, and responsible submissives must keep that in mind.

As we all know, drugs and alcohol can also affect sexual performance. On the plus side, inhibitions can be lessened under the influence of some of these substances, allowing fuller participation in fantasy play. As long as the amounts are carefully regulated so as not to be out of control, letting go of inhibitions can be a freeing experience. On the negative side, however—certainly to a great many men—drugs and alcohol can affect sexual functioning, often making erection difficult to achieve or to maintain.

9

Pain: *An Exquisite Agony**

Pain is a most natural capacity, despite a common belief that all pain is bad and that society must work to eliminate it. Pain is a system that warns of dangerous situations or of bodily damage that requires special attention. Pain is first and foremost a biological safety system.[1]

▼ ▼ ▼

A society that conceives of all love as gentle and affectionate finds difficulty in perceiving pain as enjoyable. Nor can a society which presumes all women desire abusive violence as an affirmation of their inferiority, comprehend the emotional intricacies of pain-pleasure as affectional experience between equals.[2]

▼ ▼ ▼

Given involuntarily and in an atmosphere of distrust, pain is torture, whatever the motive. But given consensually, between equals, pain can be a most incredible form of love.[3]

PHYSICAL PAIN

Are you an avid jogger, an aerobic exercise junkie, a dancer, an athlete, or just someone who spends some time every week at the gym? If you fit into any of those categories, answer the following question honestly: That stuff hurts, doesn't it? There is nothing particularly pleasant about the actual physical actions themselves, but what is pleasurable and exciting and fulfilling is the end result. That's

---

*This chapter was written and edited by JJ Madeson, and the use of the term *we* is meant to indicate that she is speaking as a member of the SM community.

why we do it: because it makes us feel so good about the process and about ourselves when we are done.

> Traditionally, sadomasochists have been viewed as people who enjoy inflicting or receiving pain. But now sex researchers are omitting the word "pain," because those involved in S&M perceive their activity as pleasurable.[4]

▼ ▼ ▼

> SM is hurting the one you love, just right!"

▼ ▼ ▼

> We're so conditioned to lovey-dovey type relations that we can't see any enjoyment in more active, exhilarating activities. We're so conditioned to all pain and pain experience as being abusive and involuntary that we can't conceive of it as a form of love.[5]

It is difficult to understand why anyone would want—even crave—pain. Freud wrestled with this seeming contradiction to his "pleasure principle" (which states that individuals will generally act in ways to increase pleasure and decrease pain), and even he found it difficult to explain how pleasure and pain could coexist.

Pain is the most confusing and misunderstood aspect of SM, and physical pain is often, but not always, a part of the SM Experience. Bondage, for example, fits well into the framework of SM without pain. It can provide a sense of being physically and sexually at the mercy of another, and thus produce psychological stimulation rather than physical pain. In fact, many SM toys (such as feathers, fur, or suede) are designed specifically to create sensations other than pain.

Not only is the issue of a desire for pain difficult for non-SMers to understand, it is sometimes even difficult for those of us involved in SM. We are all taught early in life that pain is bad and is to be avoided at all costs. When one chooses to become involved in SM, one must confront this issue; it is yet another area where guilt must be overcome.

> I'm really into pain in SM play. Having first overcome the barriers to the acceptance of SM in my life, liking pain became another issue in and of itself, another deviation from the norm that I had to learn to deal with. Now I realize that as long as it's controlled, safe, and sexual, it's okay. But this wasn't an easy place to get to. (In fact, it was at times quite painful. Giggle, giggle.)

The facts are, as many sex researchers have pointed out, that one's pain threshold rises with sexual excitement and that the physiological response to pain is similar to that of orgasm.

Pain provides a general psychophysiological arousal—anticipation, expectancy, excitement—that can increase sexual feelings. Additionally, since perception itself decreases during sexual arousal, to feel anything at all requires more intense stimulation than it otherwise would. Hence, what might appear to be painful in a nonsexual situation may well be felt during sexual arousal as pleasure or as a mixture of pain and pleasure.

> The pain–pleasure barrier could be thought of as that maximum level in intensity of a stimulus that still remains pleasurable. Toward and at that barrier, the stimulus is perceived as enjoyable; small twinges of pain are far outweighed by the pleasure. On passing through the barrier, pain overrides the pleasure. Quite obviously, emotional state of mind and predisposition both have a good deal of influence on where the barrier is positioned at any one moment.[6]

Many couples engage in some form of stimulation that could be considered painful if taken out of context. It may be biting, scratching, wrestling, even hitting. There are often times when some amount of roughness in sex play is pleasurable, and most sexually active adults have, at one time or another, suffered bruises or scratches during sex without even knowing that it was happening until later. It often occurs during a particularly passionate session of lovemaking, and the recipients of these marks do not feel the stimulation as pain; indeed what may hurt in a nonsexual context may be ignored or barely noticed in a sexual setting.

Pain is nothing more than an intense sensation, regardless of the context. The fine line between pain and pleasure can best be described by using an example from everyday life: When preparing a bath, you turn on the water and put your hand under the faucet for a moment to test the temperature; there is often an instant when you cannot truly tell if it is hot or cold.

It is this same experience we sadomasochists seek: Riding for as long as possible on the edge between pain and pleasure where the sensations are so intense one cannot tell if what they are feeling hurts or feels good—or both.

> Take one hand and hit it with the fist of the other: Which feels the most? Both feel the same force but from a different direction.[7]

In the case of SM, because the pain—whether given or received—is experienced in a sexual context, the intense sensations are *interpreted* positively, as pleasure, rather than negatively, as pain.

> The body feels stimulation; the mind interprets it. The way that the mind interprets it determines whether it's pleasure or pain.[8]

We call this phenomenon the pain/pleasure conversion, and this conversion is why SMers explain that the things which look like they must surely hurt, often do not.

> Some mysterious defensive mechanism of the body had enabled him to transcend the normal thresholds of pain. It was not that the pain was no longer present; it was. But it had become externalized. He was now merely witness to rather than victim of its . . . effects.[9]

▼ ▼ ▼

> While he knows the pain is there, he doesn't feel it in the same way [as in the real world. Another example:] Pain reduction during trance experience is particularly prevalent among individuals susceptible to hypnosis.[10]

▼ ▼ ▼

> There may be several ways in which these "higher" regions of the brain act to suppress pain. In hypnosis, for example, the subject can often still distinguish the presence of the pain but has separated the reality of the pain from its emotional contexts and its hurt.[11]

As stated earlier, the concept of obtaining pleasure from pain is more acceptable and more easily understood if one considers the pain experienced, and even sought, by the athlete or the dancer. These people train hard and push themselves to higher and higher goals of endurance despite the pain associated with their training, in order to feel the pleasure and satisfaction gained from their accomplishments. They are able to convert the painful stimulation to pleasure within the context of sport or art; without this context, the conversion would not occur and the activity would simply be painful.

> Be very clear about this: This is not a beating I'm talking about. I've been [abused and] beaten and I know the difference between pleasure and pain. This is an intensification of sensation, a heightened stimulation of certain areas and *it feels good to me*.[12]

And so it is with SM. We want to point out once again that it is not ANY pain that is eroticized in SM; it is specifically sexual stimuli. None of us purposely stub our toe or go to the dentist because we enjoy the pain. Such experiences do not fit into an erotic context (unless one is *very* creative), and they are, therefore, no more comfortable to sadomasochists than to anyone else.

> When I am dominant and in control of the scene, I am in control of the pain being inflicted on my submissive. I control how much pain, when and by what means it is inflicted. Unintentional pain or too much pain is "bad" pain, and it means I have failed in my responsibility; my control has been broken. I also have zero interest in injuring my partner since if she's injured, we can't go on playing—and THAT's bad!

In terms of SM play, we must understand the way of thinking—the mind set, if you will—that is the basis of the dominant/submissive relationship (the heart of the SM Experience): granting someone the power and the right to hurt you is an acknowledgment of that person's control.

> As play develops and opioids [brain chemicals functioning to fight pain] peak, state of mind becomes ecstatic and emotions are intensified, even exaggerated. Under the control of the top, episodes of physical and mental stress alternate with moments of intense loving and warmth.[13]

▼ ▼ ▼

> I haven't done formal meditation, but it seems to me that pain does something similar to what meditation or yoga can do, because you're focusing your body, and your mind can be free to drift and not think analytically at all.[14]

In other words, the submissive accepts the pain inflicted by the dominant as both symbolic and real proof of his or her submission. Indeed, it is just these feelings of vulnerability and powerlessness to stop the pain that are, among other things, the submissive's turn-on.

> [I] enjoy whatever [my] top does more because he does it than because of what it feels like. I get some real joy when I let go and focus on how much my master is enjoying the situation.[15]

At the same time, the feeling of power over the submissive as well as the freedom to inflict pain is the dominant's turn-on. This power exchange interaction is key to the excitement of an SM scene.

> If bondage puts a certain emphasis on mental territory, play with pain–pleasure clearly puts weight on the physical dimension. Here is a test of limits, of taking the body to its known boundaries and beyond. Here, [we] move out into new terrains and pleasures. Through physical distortion, they activate deep-seated emotion to learn of the interplay of fear and trust. And yet, despite its use of the physical, this play also makes strong statements about mental territory. It brings forth relations between mind, body and well-being; it embraces the mental euphoria at the edge of physical limits.[16]

▼ ▼ ▼

> He wants me to experience the pain; he knows it is difficult to do, and he understands that my willingness to do it is my way of demonstrating to him the love I feel.

Pain can also be a gift from one partner to the other. The dominant enjoys and is turned on by *giving* the submissive the intense experience of the pain, fully knowing that the submissive not only enjoys the stimulation but also wants to please the dominant. The submissive's *acceptance* of the pain is thus a gift to them both. This acceptance not only means "I love you enough to suffer this for you," but also acknowledges the mutual erotic turn-on the pain creates.

> My feelings about the actual physical sensation, the blow as opposed to the fantasy, are ambivalent. When I'm to receive a spanking, I both love it and dread it, seek it and fear it, feel the pleasure and feel the pain. . . .
> When I'm to deliver a spanking, my feelings are more single-minded. I feel powerful, responsible and in control, both of myself and of the situation. Afterwards, I feel very strong and very loving.
> [We] always hold each other close after a spanking. The person who's been spanked feels vulnerable and in need of warmth and comfort; the person who's delivered the spanking needs to offer strength and love. Also, the person who's done the spanking needs to be reassured that she's done a good thing even though she's hurt her lover.[17]

Some base their fantasy play on the concept of punishment and reward. Pain for the submissive in this context is something to be feared and/or avoided, but that does not mean it is devoid of erotic significance:

> I once played with a Top who had a whole series of things she wanted me to do for her—sexual things. If I did not please her, she would use a riding crop to punish me. I *hated* that crop! It really hurt! She knew that, of course, and knew I'd do whatever she asked me to do as well as I possibly could just to avoid it.

▼　▼　▼

> He has a whip I hate, and he knows it. I call it the welt-maker, and it hurts like hell. When last he used it on me, I cried and told him once again how much I feared and hated it. But I love him and I'm turned on by the fact that using it turns him on, so I endure it.

▼　▼　▼

> Breast play is one of my biggest turn-ons; I love it. Recently, though, a lover of mine would put her fingers on my nipples and *push*—real hard. Boy, does that hurt! Pulling or slapping or pinching or squeezing them feels great—but this. . . . I hate that feeling. Since she knows that, it makes things interesting, really, in terms of when and why she does it!

The important thing to understand here is that in SM, like any other sexual activity, the goal is the same: pleasure. It should also be understood that wildly flailing away with whips is neither the point nor the reality of the SM Experience. For a successful SM encounter, it is necessary to find a balance between the pain and the tenderness, the rough and the gentle. Understanding and creatively using this balance is what often distinguishes the good player from the not-so-good, the experienced from the novice.

Some sadomasochists do go beyond the biting or scratching stages of sexual pain. Physical pain in SM is caused by behaviors that range from pinches, slaps, and bites to those that may leave marks or draw blood. And there are those who, while not being specifically turned on by pain, find the marks left by whips and other toys exciting.

> I see my acceptance of and tolerance for pain as real proof of who I am, of the strength to survive that's within me.

▼　▼　▼

> I'm not particularly into pain, but I like the marks, the bruises—they signify possession, and that's a big thing for me. The marks

mean that since he has power to cause enough pain to leave marks, I must belong to him, and that sense of possession is something we both crave.

▼ ▼ ▼

The next day or so after the scene, when I'm undressed at home, I can take a look at the marks in the mirror, whatever kind they are, and it brings back a tingly memory of the scene. A little tickle that says, "Ooh, I remember THAT!"

So for people like those above, it is the result, rather than the means, that is the turn-on. An important note here is that these marks or bruises are rarely the kind that can be seen by the "outside world," neither black eyes nor swollen lips. They are usually black and blue marks on the buttocks, breasts, or other places. We are, after all, not out to shock the world; indeed, most of us wish to hide the signs of our sexual practices from the general population since the possibility of misinterpretation is so obvious. As we have seen, the price is high if these things become obvious to the outside world.

I was at a party with a guy who plays very heavy with whips and crops. We had quite a lengthy scene and my butt was really black and blue. I remembered too late that I had an appointment for a massage the next day! Needless to say, I had to reschedule it. I wouldn't have wanted to try and explain the marks; those are for my private pleasure. (The same situation could have been true if the appointment had been with a doctor.)

Often it is the context, rather than the physical sensations or even the marks themselves, that is exciting.

You get the mind of the right person in the proper space, play . . . a little, and whammo! It's incredible where you can go, just writhing in the sweetness of it all.[18]

▼ ▼ ▼

Whether you are being dominant or submissive, the things being done in an SM scene are not nearly as important as the "head space" of the players in terms of dominance or submission while they're being done. That place in your mind is really what's exciting and beautiful; marks are irrelevant.

To some, of course, the pain *is* as exciting as the context; most often, however, the two are so intertwined that they are impossible to separate . . . like pain/pleasure!

Just as runners train to run longer and longer distances, we sadomasochists sometimes try to increase our tolerance for sexual pain, either by increasing the intensity of the pain, withstanding the same intensity for a longer period of time, or both. There are many motivations behind the desire to expand tolerances for pain just as there are in pushing limits.

For example, since two people are rarely matched exactly in their SM desires, experience, and capabilities, one partner may wish to increase his or her tolerance for pain in order to play at the more intense levels desired by the other.

> SM is the humiliation of discovering that your new slave is far more experienced than you are!

Gradual expansion of the intensity or duration of the painful stimulation is often seen as growth in SM and/or as a continuing demonstration of the submissive's trust and love for the dominant.

> Are You Proud of Me?
>
> I want you to be.
> If you are, then I feel proud.
>
> I want to endure your pain
> as quietly as a butterfly.
>
> My endurance is my gift to you, my love.
>
> Just to do easy things
> is too easy.
> Unless it's hard to do,
> it doesn't prove anything—
>   to either of us.
>
> And with my acceptance
> of the gift of pain you give me,
> Then you know . . . I love you.

Another example:

> I had an experience with a lover that both excited and frightened me. We were involved in an SM scene and he was using his hand

to spank me. The feelings were thrillingly intense. At some point, however, what he was doing began to hurt—really hurt. I could no longer experience the pain as pleasure. We had reached a limit.

I tried to crawl away from the pain, but there was an instant, then, when I realized that he was quite aware of the fact that he was hurting me; he knew he was pushing me beyond my limit for pain. And he knew that I knew what he was doing. It was an almost eerie telepathic communication.

At that moment, my resistance ceased. My abdication of power to my dominant became complete. I stopped fighting the pain (fighting it makes it worse, by the way) and let it wash over me like a wave. The frightening part, then and now, was the sexual excitement created by the real pain and by our mutual recognition that he knew he was causing real pain and did not stop.

His dominance had become a reality; he was truly in control. He was experiencing an intense release of energy strictly for his own pleasure; we both felt it. He knew he was hurting me, yet he did not stop. He had called my submissive bluff: His pleasure, not mine, became paramount. He was saying, "I want this. Do it for me." I responded by accepting the pain and the reality of my submission in its truest sense.

I had given up the power. The safety was in the fact that I had given it up to someone who cared about me, someone who was sure enough of himself and his own sense of stability to know that he would not go too far. He knew he was trusted, and he accepted the responsibility that comes with the gift of trust.

Similar, again, to a runner training to beat his personal best, some of us push our pain limits for reasons of competition: the desire to surpass others or even ourselves. Sometimes, when one has a "reputation" for taking heavy pain, to do any less is disappointing. There are also goals that one sets for oneself. One man, for example, enjoys the use of clothespins on his body and keeps track of how many are used each time in an effort to surpass the last time. With the help of his dominant, they are pushing his limits.

PSYCHOLOGICAL PAIN

It is possible to have an SM experience completely without physical pain, one in which dominance and submission are acknowledged in other ways; this can be called psychological pain, and it includes feelings such as uncertainty, apprehension, shame, embarrassment, humiliation, powerlessness, and fear.

The most common component of SM's psychological pain is humiliation, where the Top embarrasses the submissive by accentuating his (or her) helplessness. For example, submissives may be humiliated by being made to lick their dominant's boots or kiss the dominant's buttocks. Female dominants sometimes "demean" their male partners by forcing them to wear female clothing (a prevalent theme in SM fantasies and literature), or by giving them tasks or chores to do which, of course, raise the possibility of "misbehaving," necessitating "punishment." It is most important to note that NONE of the concepts here are used maliciously and are, once again, strictly consensual.

Psychological pain is probably the most subjective area of SM play, for it is truly in the mind of the beholder. The subjectivity exists because what humiliates, intimidates, or embarrasses me, what makes me fearful, may not affect you in the least. And vice versa. Also, what is humiliating one night might not seem that way the next time we do the same thing, just as something that hurts tonight may not even, under different circumstances, hurt tomorrow.

For example, being told to stay on your knees in a corner of a room during a party would be humiliating to some people and just boring to others. Being naked in a room filled with fully dressed people (an experience known to most submissives) can be a humiliating experience, creating feelings of exposure and vulnerability.

While there is an element of humiliation inherent in the dominant/submissive relationship itself in that the focus is on the vulnerability of the bottom and the intimacy of the top's power and control, there are, in addition, other types of humiliation play.

Pride and self-esteem are two character traits upon which humiliation play impacts, and both qualities can be diminished during such play. Since pride and self-esteem are integral parts of what makes us who we are, it is crucial to express the caring and loving feelings that exist between those playing this way both before and after such a scene, allowing a nurturing, a healing, and a return to the equal status between the partners.

Being able to handle humiliation is often a sign of the strength of character of the submissive who participates in such scenes, for one must be very sure of one's own personal strengths to come out the other end of humiliation play with character intact; and one must also be sure, too, of the respect one's dominant has for them. If this knowledge is missing, humiliation scenes become real turn-offs.

Fear and teasing are two other aspects of psychological pain, and both are issues that require a great deal of trust between the partners when they come into play. Fear may be a turn-on but terror is not; it is too real and goes well beyond eroticism. But when the submissive can trust that the dominant will not actually do the things he or she may threaten to do, the partners can then play with the fear.

> When he holds that burning candle near my breast, I am terrified. It's *so* close. But I know that he will not burn me. He'll come close but he won't do it. We've talked this through, and I am secure in that knowledge. Because I know this, I can relax and really get into the fear. I can scream or plead or beg, be excited or frightened by the possibilities. It's fun, though, at the time to believe that he will do it. It is an illusion that makes our play all that more real.

▾　▾　▾

> She knew that fear was useless, that he would do what he wished, that the decision was his, that he left nothing possible to her except the thing she wanted most—to submit.[19]

Playing with fear gives the submissive the opportunity to play the "no, no, please don't" part of the fantasy—the "against my will" or the "victim" role—that increases the fear, the vulnerability, and the turn-on.

The "no, no, please don't" fantasy often plays a part in another intense but common aspect of SM play: acting out a nonconsensual scenario. Kidnap, rape, and torture are common fantasies and acting them out during SM play is no more real than in the movies. With underlying and acknowledged consensuality, these fantasy games can be exciting and erotic.

> He'd always threatened to give me away to a gang, to let them do what they wanted with me 'cuz he knew the idea turned me on. It was a hot fantasy. So one day during our play, he blindfolded me, and a bunch of guys (all friends, I found out later) came into the room. They tied me up, put me in a van and drove away. When they stopped the van, they threw me down on the floor, fondled me, slapped me; my lover (again, I didn't know it at that time) had sex with me and some others made me go down on them. I screamed, I cried, I begged. I really felt like a victim, but I knew my lover was there and had set this all up; I was never in any real danger, and so the actress in me emerged, and we all played our roles to the hilt. Finally, they drove me back to the house, dumped me in the garage, still blindfolded and now quite naked, and left me there. I was exhausted—but boy, was it fun!

One of the most intensely humiliating "loss-of-control" fantasies popular among some SMers is water sports. Urinating on a submissive or giving an enema and forcing one to retain it are humiliating experiences. Taking control over bladder and bowel functions is a way of demonstrating one's dominance; allowing another to exercise such control is a demonstration of submission. These activities reinforce feelings of humiliation and create the experience of "delicious shame."

Even orgasm is an example of a physically out-of-control experience that can be turned into humiliation during SM play by a dominant's references, for example, at a party as to how embarrassing it will feel to be forced into orgasm in a room full of people.

> Even when we first start playing, she's wet. She doesn't have control over that; her body does it without her, and we both love that. But if I mention it to her by saying something like, "God, you're an animal, aren't you? We haven't even started to play and you're soaking wet already. What a little sex junkie you are!" that humiliates her. It also makes her even wetter.

Another similar fantasy is infantilism, a humiliation scenario where the bottom is dressed in diapers and where the main props are cribs, pacifiers, toilet training, and punishment (with whips and other SM toys). While these activities had been more widespread, AIDS and other sexually transmitted diseases have greatly lessened their popularity.

10

~~~

Meeting Others
*We're Not in Kansas Anymore, Toto!**

For many SM beginners, a visit to an SM professional is their first and safest foray into the SM world. There, they have the opportunity to explore their fantasies and/or desires before any SM play begins, to discuss rules and safety precautions, and to reach agreements as to the style and the activities of the scene to come.

Most SM professionals are women and are usually, but not always, dominant; they are referred to as mistress, dominatrix or "pro doms." Their clients are almost all male, although submissive women, especially those who are either lesbian or bisexual, can visit mistresses who specify that they will play with women. A one-hour session with a professional mistress usually costs between $100 and $200. Such sessions take place at either the mistress' private "playroom," which is often shared by two or three other women for use with their own clients, or at an organized facility where a variety of "dungeons" are available for use by mistresses and their clients. There are few such organized facilities still in existence, so most professionals work out of their homes or share a condominium apartment set up specifically for SM sessions.

Some facilities employ submissives (or switches), usually women, who are available for sessions as well. Since submission carries with

---

*This chapter was written and edited by JJ Madeson, and the use of the term *we* is meant to indicate that she is speaking as a member of the SM community.

it a greater possibility of injury, the rules for these types of sessions are often more stringent in order to protect the submissive. Although there are occasionally men who are SM pros, most, if not all, of their clients are also men (and often, both are gay).

Some professionals—again, not all—enjoy SM activities in their private lives, and they are considered by many to be better qualified and more sensitive to their clients' needs than those for whom SM is only a job. Professional dominants rarely see clients socially, both to assure confidentiality and to keep business separate from personal attachments. There are exceptions, and some very deep and personal relationships have formed between mistress and client.

Professionals meet clients by advertising in local, regional, or national sexually oriented publications in addition to word-of-mouth referrals. The ads are usually specific as to what areas of SM are the specialty of the dominants, whether they will accept men and/or women as clients, and whether or not they are willing to provide sessions for novices (most are).

> Redhead in leather enjoys mind and body control, erotic torture, and tease. Slave training. Baby scenes, panty and foot fetish, humiliation, spanking, discipline. Large private well-equipped space. Houseboy/slave/maid auditions available. Ask if you qualify. Newcomers welcome. Limits respected. No sex.

▼　▼　▼

> MISTRESS MYSTERY makes reality better than fantasy (and vice versa!) Playful yet commanding. Petite yet intense in Leather and Lace. . . .

Most SM professionals clearly specify that there is "no sex" (usually defined as intercourse, fellatio, cunnilingus, or manipulation to orgasm) during the session. This may surprise the uninitiated, but the "no sex" rule is used to protect everyone from disease and the professional from possible charges of prostitution. If a male client wishes an orgasm as part of the scenario, the play is choreographed so that he can masturbate to achieve release. This is an important concept, for the most common question about professional SM has always been: "Is it prostitution?"

In *Dominant Women, Submissive Men* (1984; republished as *Erotic Power*), sociologist Gini Scott discusses the issue this way:

> Mistresses and others in the scene make a clear distinction [between professional domination and prostitution] . . . arguing that the mistress doesn't provide sex. "It's not prostitution," one mistress as-

serted. "I don't have sex. If the man has an orgasm, it's because he causes it; I don't do that."

Others distinguish between mistresses and prostitution in terms of power, since the mistress has the power to decide whether the client will achieve sexual release and in what way. As one professional argued, "A prostitute has sex with anyone. [She] has no choice." Still another stated that "when a woman is a prostitute, she has no control. The customer pays her and she does what he wants. But when I have a client, he is not buying a sexual object. He is the object and I do what I want; I have the power and control."

Clients, too, distinguish dominance from prostitution: One man says that "although I'm buying sexual services, I'm also giving my power to the mistress to use; *she* has the choice of whether to give me sexual satisfaction or not. Sure, I'd like it," he says, "maybe I even expect it since I'm paying, but in the fantasy game we are playing, I don't have the right to demand it, and I know it. My fulfillment is up to her."

SOCIALLY

There are other entrances to the SM subculture. Most look for partners in those places where finding others with the same interests is most likely: SM organizations, private and/or public parties, personal ads in SM magazines, and through friends already involved.

Some may try to introduce non-SM friends and lovers to SM but for the most part

> it's just easier to hook up with others at SM functions. Bringing a straight lover into SM is a very scary, very risky business. Chances are that once subtle hints become more direct, they [whether men or women] will run away—fast.

A more focused method for meeting SM-interested partners is by placing or answering "personal ads." This is a popular starting point for establishing SM contacts, especially for those who do not live in areas where organized groups exist. Opinions on this option vary, but many feel that

> we are largely restricted in means of meeting compatible lovers and sex partners because of the secretiveness imposed on us by a disapproving society so we often resort to "sex ads," advertisements in

certain publications that contain coded information concerning what we enjoy and what sort of partner we are seeking.

The safest place to advertise or respond to personal ads is via SM organization newsletters where the ads need not be subtle. The safeguards in such advertising is that the advertisers are usually known to the group that produces these publications. Reports to the editors of these publications of dangerous or unsafe encounters with advertisers will usually result in denial of further ads, for the SM network protects its members.

The type of advertising varies with the kind of publication. In the San Francisco Bay Area, the *Spectator* (formerly the famed *Berkeley Barb*) is a sexually oriented weekly paper with a large "personals" section dealing predominantly with sexual interest; there is no need for subtlety here. One section of the classifieds is called "De Sade" and, obviously enough, it is here that a great number of SMers, including many professional dominants, advertise.

There is a series of nationally-distributed magazines published by Los Angeles-based B&D Enterprises that contain, along with stories, letters and photographs, a multitude of ads specifically geared toward finding either SM partners or SM penpals. Many ads are from couples looking for additional partners (singles or other couples) for SM play.

In yet another newspaper, most classified ads are aimed more towards relationships than sex, but it is here, too, that many SMers attempt to meet others. Because the publication is not openly sexual and because of the taboos surrounding SM, many ads contain "buzz words" that, it is hoped, will be recognized and understood specifically by other sadomasochists. The "buzz words" have been italicized in the following examples:

TEACH ME THE *ROPES*: White male, 28, attractive, intelligent, creative, well-traveled, sometimes professional, usually humorous—looking for an attractive *high-heeled*, high energy female for mutual *fantasy*, fun, friendship and frolicsome flirtation.

▼   ▼   ▼

DO YOU UNDERSTAND when I say that I am a petite white female, independently *submissive*, together, cute but lonely, looking for a white male who can be *dominant* but gentle, loving/caring/open/giving. The ideal *Top* will be 35+, attractive, know the *"scene,"* secure/sensitive/creative with love and time to share—and a man who understands this ad. Tell me what you see and who you are.

The authoress of the above ad says:

> I received an answer to my ad from a guy who DID understand! It was one of the hottest letters I'd ever read; it really turned me on, and I wrote back an equally hot, appropriately submissive, response. I never heard from the guy again. I admit to being really disappointed. Several years later, there was an ad in an SM group newsletter from a submissive man looking for a dominant woman to play with. His name and description made me realize that it was the same guy! I wrote a heavy dominant letter this time, ordering him to respond, but not giving away my secret. I wanted revenge! Needless to say, I never got a response that time either, so obviously I was dealing with a "letter freak." Too bad—it might have been fun.

▾ ▾ ▾

> When I was brand new in the SM scene, I answered an ad that asked, among other things, for someone familiar with toe clips. I assumed this was some kind of SM toy unfamiliar to me, and answered the ad with a letter saying I wasn't specifically familiar with toe clips, but had played with nipple clips and other sorts of SM clamp-type toys. The guy called about a week later, and we had a wonderfully hysterical phone conversation in which I leaned that toe clips are used by people into bicycling! I sure misunderstood that clue, but the guy thought my response intriguing enough to warrant a call. We laughed over it and chalked it up to experience!

A few more examples:

> MILD-MANNERED sensitive *subservient* single man, 51, seeks *strong-willed* women for permanent *role reversal* relationship. If you want to *wear the pants* in your family and *make* your partner do the housework and *wait on you*, please write. . . .

▾ ▾ ▾

> Young, slender, *compliant* male wants relationship with *forceful* female. . . .

Because SM interests are so diverse, social signals have developed to give prospective partners in social situations an idea of what their interests are. As noted by Thomas Weinberg in his 1987 article in the respected *Journal of Sex Research:*

> Symbolism is a strong element in the SM subculture. Within that world, certain elements, such as, for example, particular articles of

clothing, take on special meanings which are culturally produced, learned and reinforced. This symbolism is illustrated in SM magazines which picture SM participants in standardized costumes, most often in leather or rubber garments. Women are often clothed in tight corsets, garter belts and high boots. The meaning of this apparel for participants in the SM subculture has not yet been [fully] explored, although there is an apparent consensus within that community that goes beyond its special significance for the individual.[1]

As noted, leather has often been a sign of involvement in SM, but in recent years we find this accoutrement as a high fashion costume, used by many well-known designers of women's clothing, Gianni Versace, among others. Additionally, the "punk rock" enthusiasts of the 1980s adopted not only leather clothing, but metal studs, dog collars, and handcuffs as their own, making what had been traditional SM costuming "the rage" in other areas of fashion and advertising. This presented difficulties for SM people, for they could no longer be sure whether the person wearing leather or sporting similar signals was truly into SM or was just being fashionable!

> Leather itself is the ultimate metaphor, symbol of our animal nature and the dark side of our souls.[2]

▾ ▾ ▾

> I'm tired of people who see leather as a fashion. It's my second skin. I'll be damned happy when the fashion world tires of studded arm bands and slave collars and discovers something else. Although these styles have been pretty popular for a long time, what I wear isn't fashion. It's me being me.[3]

Since approaches to others can be misread, this difference is important in seeking SM partners.

> Some sadomasochists deliberately look scary. They are giving signals for rough games, which they know how to play and are ready for. If you're not ready or don't know what you're doing, keep away! They take themselves seriously—and so should you.

In addition to traditional associations with black leather and other fetish clothing, a system of key and handkerchief codes has been adopted (primarily by gay men) to communicate specific interests to others. The key code is simply a set of keys worn on either the right or left side of the belt to communicate whether the person is dominant (left) or submissive (right). It is interesting to note that originally, the East Coast tradition was that the left side indicated dominance while the right indicated submission; West Coast codes were exactly the opposite. Now, however, the East Coast system has won out and is internationally recognized.

A little more complex is the handkerchief code, a system that has evolved wherein the color, pattern, and sometimes even the material of the handkerchief worn in a back pocket represents specific sexual activities in which its wearer is interested, and its placement (left or right pocket) again indicates dominant/submissive orientation as it relates to the particular activity.

For example, a black handkerchief worn on the left side indicates the wearer is a "heavy" (very intense) top, while the same handkerchief worn on the right means a heavy bottom; a teal handkerchief on the left means the man enjoys giving "cock and ball torture"; on the right, it signifies a bottom who enjoys receiving it.

Whatever the outward signals, experienced SMers will ask for further clarification of the codes' significance, both for safety's sake and to avoid the need later to say, "Yes, but I thought . . . "

Discussions about SM preferences, while integral to any SM scene, also act as icebreakers in social situations. Indeed, in some leather bars, potential partners may spend hours getting to know one another before even establishing who will be dominant, who submissive. They are discovering one another's uniqueness as a basis for their SM play. People who will take the time to discover and appreciate your unique personality [and interests] can probably be trusted; offers of instant play are suspect.

RELATIONSHIPS

In the context of a relationship, I think SM helps to bring us closer together as we share our most intimate fantasies. To make our activity more pleasurable, we must communicate well—and not only about sexual matters. This openness, I believe, enhances both the trust between us and our ability to share intimate but nonsexual parts of ourselves. The process of communicating our feelings, by conceptualizing and verbalizing our feelings, helps us look more deeply within ourselves so we can understand ourselves and each other better.

SM is a nontraditional sexual lifestyle and many of us find that, having overcome one societal taboo, it is easier to overcome others.

Thus, the parameters society has set for relationships, such as conventional marriage and monogamy, may be less important to those of us who have already departed from the norm by our choice of lifestyle. To a certain extent, too, because those involved in SM infrequently relate intimately to those who are uninvolved, the parameters and stereotypes simply do not apply.

While SM and its practitioners are generally viewed as "oddities" (to be nice) or "perverts" (to be judgmental), the truth is that, except for our sexual interests, relationships and friendships within the SM community function no differently from those on the "outside," and emotional involvement is just as prevalent and just as necessary in SM situations as in any other sexual liaison.

Relationships, whether social or sexual, vary from the casual one-night stand of sexual/SM play to friendships to long-term commitments to marriage, and the pros and cons of such relationships are similar regardless of who the people are.

> The exploration is itself liberating ... While the dynamics of SM
> may reinforce the categorization of sex and sex roles, I think it is
> more likely to break them down. People have an opportunity to
> be more aware of the elements of dominance and submission in
> all relationships.[4]

Let us look now into a few kinds of relationships as they exist within the SM world (and in any other social milieu, for that matter).

Casual Encounters

As with many sexually active adults, there are many sadomasochists—gay, bi, and straight—who find casual SM exciting and fun. Such encounters offer many things: the excitement of not knowing what's going to happen, the thrill of discovery about a new partner, the "conquest" of someone new, the advantages of anonymity, the fantasy of being taken by a stranger and, for some, the possibility that casual meetings can lead to longer relationships. In contrast, those who wish to avoid commitment often see a casual encounter as having less chance of creating involvement.

The key problem with all casual sexual arrangements, SM or otherwise, is that they are potentially dangerous. As John Lee observed in his 1979 article entitled "The Social Organization of Sexual Risk"[5] and as seems rather obvious, "those who seek casual sexual encounters with strangers (whether gay or non-gay) put themselves at risk." Lee called this risk the "Looking for Mr.Goodbar" syndrome, based on the book and movie of the same title, where a woman meets a man in a bar, goes home with him, and is stabbed to death during sex.

While it might seem that the risks of casual sexual encounters increase when the type of activity sought is sadomasochistic, Lee observed that "an examination of the SM subculture and its institutions and participants revealed a surprisingly low level of reported incidents where anyone was thoroughly frightened or physically harmed."

Although Lee studied Toronto's gay SM community, the same observation appears to be valid within the heterosexual and homosexual SM communities in this country. Both Spengler (1977) and Moser (1979) found that such injuries, as well as more extreme and dangerous SM practices, occur with minimal frequency. Further, as we saw in chapter 8, there are many safety measures built into SM society that serve to lessen the risks of any SM encounter.

Another kind of safety concern has, in the past few decades, taken hold in the sexually active community. The incidents of casual sex, SM and/or straight, is declining rapidly due to the spread of sexually transmitted diseases, most particularly AIDS. While AIDS once struck most often in the gay community, legitimate fear of the disease has now reached deep into the bisexual and heterosexual community as well, and casual sex appears to be much less prevalent.

Committed Relationships

The dating process and the desire for permanent relationships are no less valued within the SM community than in any other, where generally, people look for partners with whom they are compatible—intellectually, emotionally, and sexually. These goals are shared by those of us in the SM community, but we have an additional consideration in that we seek partners with the reciprocal SM role (dominant or submissive) and we must look for others with similar SM interests (bondage, pain, water sports, etc.) and one who plays at a similar level of intensity.

> When two people are alone together, and one of them is naked and tied up, and the other is standing over them holding whips and other torture implements, this is not the time to have a serious mismatch of expectations.[6]

Because of these specific needs, most SM practitioners seek partners within the SM community. It is not imperative, of course, that we settle down only with another SMer; the decision depends on how committed one feels to an SM lifestyle. Most couples in committed relationships seem to believe that "if push comes to shove," the relationship would take precedence over the SM. This is borne out by our observation of relationships where the SM had to be discontinued due to medical problems.

Once established, SM relationships go through the same trials and tribulations as any other with the additional acknowledged understanding that SM is never a means by which to vent anger. It is far more meaningful as a deep coming together when feelings are mutually positive and is frequently used (as is sex in the "outside" world) to make up.

Although studies have claimed that there are very few ongoing live-in relationships between SM people and that, without societal supports, such relationships are usually of short duration, the view from the inside is much different. Interaction with the SM community has revealed hundreds, if not thousands, of live-in, married, or deeply committed relationships, heterosexual, gay, and lesbian. While the stability, length, and depth of commitment in SM relationships have not been "officially" studied, we have seen that sadomasochists, just like anyone else, successfully maintain long-term and/or permanent relationships.

Interestingly, we point out that it is both difficult and unusual for an SM couple (live-in or not) to maintain their SM roles full-time. The reality is that most have jobs and straight lives to lead, and the intensity of SM play is, therefore (like sexual activity in most relationships), often reserved for sexual or erotic occasions.

> I do play more now—as often as possible, in fact! I resent the time I can't play, because it's very special to share this kind of sexuality. It's turned out to be more than just sex play: it's the way I want to lead my life. The only reason my husband and I don't devote ourselves full-time to living our SM fantasies is that, unfortunately, we have to go to work sometimes, if only for rent money, food and new toys!

We have known a few couples who have attempted to maintain their SM roles on a full-time basis when they were together. Most found this arrangement detrimental to the relationship because, in the long run, if the partners submerge their individuality in favor of a fantasy role, they may be removing from the relationship not only opportunities to spend time together just relaxing and being themselves, but more importantly, the unique and multifaceted personalities that had originally attracted the partners to one another.

Some of us occasionally plan an extended period of time, perhaps a long weekend or a vacation, in which we do try to maintain our SM roles full-time. This is both fun and challenging to our creativity, and without the everyday hassles of the "real" world, the partners can truly indulge in the fullness of their fantasies.

In a variety of ways, then, SM is woven into the lives of those who practice it, limited only by the bounds of time and imagination.

One marriage, for example, works this way:

> Our life is not always a scene, but we do incorporate as much SM into it as we can. On weekday evenings, whether we play or not (depending on our energy levels), I come home from work and become the Mistress. He comes home, puts on his collar and becomes Slave.
>
> We've recently drawn up a contract that formalizes my control over him. It's my game and I make the rules. I can change the rules whenever I want and he has no input. He likes this more formal arrangement, and I find that the contract gives me a lot more confidence in my dominance; it's a growing experience. This particular contract expires in three months, and we'll see then whether or not we are interested in renewing it, with what restrictions and for how long.
>
> Usually, we play most of the weekend. He comes home on Friday, showers and puts on his collar. We play for a while, but we're both often tired from the work week so that scene ends pretty early. On Saturday morning, he has tasks to do and punishment if he doesn't do them properly. He must wear his collar unless he's out in public; he's always in role; and when he finishes his tasks, he asks, "Mistress, do you have anything else for me to do?"
>
> Saturday night we almost always play, either with friends or alone. I specify the time; I tell him what to wear, how to prepare and set up the play space. Our play can last anywhere from three to five hours.
>
> He serves me breakfast in bed on Saturday and Sunday mornings. When we have guests and if he's not directly involved in play, he serves drinks, empties ashtrays and sits on the floor beside me if he's not otherwise occupied. Sunday we play, too, on and off during the day and evening. On Monday morning, I take his collar off, and he goes to work.
>
> He does get an occasional night out but everything must be cleared and negotiated through me. He can't play with anybody without my permission. Basically, I have total control over his life except when he's at work, and this is exactly how he likes it.

The contract takes the decisions away from him but not the responsibility. He has *given* me the power to make decisions for him; the contract was signed voluntarily. A dominant can't really force a submissive to give up power and responsibility, but when I hear women at work bitch because they can't get their husbands to help with the dishes, I think, "If only they knew how good they could have it!"

Some SMers see their relationships as deeper than "vanilla" ones because, by honestly and openly sharing sexual fantasies, we learn more about each other and can relate on a deeper and more intimate level.

I have never felt the same kind of closeness and trust in non-SM relationships as I have with SM friends and lovers. We have shared the crossing of boundaries of socially acceptable behavior and it's magical. It's great to do what we do; we don't have to pretend and fake and lie like our parents seemed to show us was the only way. We can really touch others and they can reach inside us and we can do in a positive light all those things that we're not supposed to do. We gain a lot from the experience.

▾ ▾ ▾

I'd been out in the gay world for many years before I became associated with the leather scene. I couldn't believe the sense of warmth and openness that existed. Of people who liked each other as a people. Of friendships that went on for years.[7]

▾ ▾ ▾

To the Columnist: You know who I love? I love everybody in SM! I love tops because they are so friendly and beligerant! I love bottoms because they are so majestically servile! I love the lesbians because they are *women*! I love the gay men because they are so cool! I love the non-gendered sex radicals because their favorite role is that they don't have a role! I love the high-esteem people because they are such fabulous role models for the low self-esteem people! I love the low self-esteem people because they have the best excuses! I love slave auctions because they're a shopper's paradise! I even love the support groups because they are so—supportive![8]

While many couples within the SM community are in traditional marriages, there are also less traditional arrangements that are just as deep and just as committed. Importantly, because such alternative arrangements sometimes involve more than two people, participants in such relationships have adapted and restricted their sexual behaviors to conform to today's safety considerations.

From an SM man:

> I have a committed three-way relationship, myself and two women.
> We call it a group marriage or triad. We have all been married at
> other times in our lives (not to each other), yet our feelings for each
> other and for the relationship itself are deeper than during any of
> our marriages. We are more "married," more committed, than ever
> before. Our relationship is permanent and while we live separately
> at the moment, we are remodeling a house we can all share. In the
> meantime, we spend a lot of time together and in various combina-
> tions of the three of us and our other friends.

▾　▾　▾

> My wife and I love each other deeply and have been married for more
> than 10 years. We are unusual, though, in that our sexual styles
> have never really meshed (although we both enjoy SM as part of our
> sexuality), and we have chosen to maintain a nonsexual relationship.
> Our commitment to each other, however, is deep, permanent and
> spiritual. Though separate, sexuality remains a joy in our lives and
> so our marriage is open sexually (with specific restrictions relating
> to health) and we both see others. We generally get along well with
> our spouse's other lovers and often attend social functions as a group.

▾　▾　▾

> My husband and I have a secure open marriage and we are both into
> SM. I don't switch at all, so he's always submissive to me when we
> play. He does switch, though, and so his dominant needs were being
> stifled in our sexual encounters. So now he has a submissive lover,
> and they get together about once a week. This way, we both get what
> we need in terms of our SM life, and none of this diminishes our
> commitment and love for each other.

One man has yet another arrangement: The woman with whom he
lives is not into SM at all, and so their sex life is strictly "vanilla." At
the same time, they have an open, nonmonogamous relationship and
she knows that the other women he sees are into SM as well. He has
the best of both worlds: a wonderful home and sexual life with a
sprinkling of SM for variety.

On the other hand, there are those whose SM lives exist in complete
secrecy, unknown even to spouses.

> My wife knows nothing about my interest in SM. Our sex life is fine
> but I like the variety SM offers, and it is simply not something she
> would understand. I wish it were otherwise, that she could accept

and participate in SM activities with me. But I do go—alone—to SM parties occasionally. I can't stay long— just long enough to catch up with friends, maybe play a little; then I must leave. I also need to make sure that my play leaves no bruises—that would be too difficult to explain at home! It is a tough double life but SM is a deep part of who I am, and I can't just ignore it.

Also:

> I was brought up to believe in the idea of traditional marriage, and until I discovered SM, that was the only option. Once into SM, however, I began to learn about alternative lifestyles. Many of the people I know in the SM community have something other than a traditional marriage but seem just as contented—if not more so—than what I've seen of conventional marriage. I am now in a committed relationship and while my partner is not monogamous, I still prefer the monogamous path. I occasionally play SM with others, but intercourse is shared only with my partner.

As in the last example, some will share SM play with others but reserve certain activities for special partners.

> We both play with others but one of our most intense and intimate SM activities is temporary piercing, and that we reserve strictly for each other. We have also agreed that markings such as permanent pierces or tattooing, if we decide to do it at all, will not involve others because we see these experiences as signs of our commitment to each other.

So some of us are totally monogamous in all ways; some do SM play with others than their "significant other," but reserve intercourse only for each other, an arrangement becoming more popular as the AIDS crisis continues. To paraphrase a TV ad for condoms, "I'll do a lot for SM and sex, but they're not worth dying for."

SM PARTIES

Some time ago, I attended a discreet private party in a nearby town, which was held in a cavernous but romantically illuminated hall. Off against one far wall, a naked man lay belly-down on a massage table while a woman in a white lace corset striped his twitching buttocks with a willow switch. In a corner, with a red collar buckled around her neck and her hands tied behind her back, a woman knelt to kiss the stiletto pumps on another woman's feet and shivered when a pointed toe was pushed up against her lips. Around a bend in the wall, another woman lay spread-eagled in a sling, her wrists and ankles cuffed to thick chains that held the four corners of the wide leather pouch suspended from fat ring bolts in the ceiling, while a man wearing only a condom rocked her gently back and forth, pulling her down to the base of his cock, then pushing her away again.

There was a table against the wall full of condoms, dental dams, finger cots, latex gloves, lubricants, and paper towels. Nearby, one man stood bound by intricate rope designs to a pair of six-by-six uprights as two others clad in black leather from their military caps to their motorcycle boots alternately slapped the cheeks of his ass with paddles and their hands, laughing and joking as he squealed and roared and begged for just a moment of mercy.

An hour later, the woman in the collar and the man who had been caned were lounging around a dining-room table full of cold cuts, cheeses, crackers, raw vegetables, fruits, cookies, coffee, tea, and soft drinks. They smiled and spoke quietly, occasionally nuzzling the women who had topped them. Near the uprights, the man who had been spanked enthusiastically praised his friends' abilities to keep their paddles swinging even when their arms were tired. Meanwhile, he wielded a paddle of his own upon one of their bare bottoms, and the woman in the sling still swung back and forth before her partner like some antebellum belle in her hammock rocking in a sultry summer breeze.[9]

Most sadomasochists are very social and parties are frequent, whether group-sponsored or private. Some get-togethers are strictly social, some specifically for play, but most are a combination of both. Whatever one's sexual preference may be, sharing time with others in the community offers relief from the secrecy of an SM lifestyle.

SM behavior at parties can be overt (that is, whipping, caning, etc., done in the open) or more subtle (by significant costuming and/or the way in which the partners relate to each other even if they don't play). Party invitations almost always specify whether or not there will be play, alleviating the problem of offending guests who might be uncomfortable with overt SM play.

An SM party is (almost) like any other—people talk about things they have in common, brag or complain about their children, share potluck dishes, etc. Usually an area is set aside for socializing so friendships can be renewed and new friends made. If the party is group-sponsored, a short informational program may begin the evening.

Although many organized SM groups have a specific role orientation that guides the play at parties, there are occasions where the *whole*

SM community—gay, lesbian, bi, hetero, Top, bottom, or in between— can meet and play together in a high-energy, fun atmosphere. The advantage to such mixed parties is that these events are usually private rather than group-sponsored and this can promote a freer atmosphere in which to share and explore the vast and varied energies that come together. The community gathers at these functions to meet, play, share ideas and social time.

Beginning in the evening and lasting well into the early morning hours, some of these parties have truly become exciting, highly anticipated "events." The cost of admission varies depending on whether the party is group-sponsored or private, and most private functions are free. Either way, volunteers take on the responsibilities of providing food, drinks, setup and cleanup.

The key to a successful party—any party—is people.

One or two wrong people at a party can ruin it for everyone. When I'm playing at a party, I'm very vulnerable; I'm exposing my deepest erotic impulses to the eyes of other people. I'm quite naked, both physically and emotionally. This makes for a situation of heightened awareness, of very intense feelings, so any act of rudeness or crass insensitivity on the part of another person can really destroy my mood and my desire to continue to participate.

▼ ▼ ▼

The selection of people for a party is critical. I don't want to be subjected to the sexually aroused state of some unpleasant individual whom I wouldn't even want to be around in a bar drinking beer. That's why private parties are more fun for me because I know the mix of the people specifically invited will be better all around.

▼ ▼ ▼

Their parties are the best I've ever attended; they're so wonderful that they have set the standard for everyone's parties! Everyone there knows exactly how to play in public, how to conduct themselves with courtesy and respect for other people. And these are very hot people, experienced players who really know how to put on a good scene. It's a perfect mix.

▼ ▼ ▼

Some people just don't get it when it comes to establishing and maintaining the proper mood at a party. People sometimes stand around a play area (when someone's actually playing there) and talk about the most inappropriate subjects. The last thing I want is to be stark naked at a public party, on my hands and knees before my Mistress, wearing handcuffs and ankle restraints, and have to listen to some people talking about their damn jobs while I'm trying to get my head into bottom space. I mean, really, why are they there?

Dress varies at SM parties and is often dependent on role. Dominant men usually dress casually and in black. Submissive men dress according to their own style and their dominants' wishes.

Women, whether dominant or submissive, take the opportunity at these events to *really* dress up: Long formal dresses, custom leather wear, special jewelry, high heels, garters, stockings, and heels. SM parties are wonderful fashion shows and part of the fun is to see the imaginative and creative costumes.

Over the years, I've observed a tendency for a number of SM people—but by no means all—to create a kind of conformity in the manner of dress. There's always an abundance of black leather, black clothes, black toys—black everything! I find myself wanting to see a greater diversity in color, fashion, and theme, etc.

▼ ▼ ▼

I get so tired of dressing for play in all black or all white, and I really make an effort to buy or concoct party outfits that contain at least some elements of some other color. By now, it's become a really creative challenge, and one that pays off in compliments from my friends.

Most party guests are expected to arrive in "regular" clothing, protecting neighbors and preserving confidentiality.

When I dress for play, it's like a matador's ritual before a fight. I change from an ordinary person to a glowing, growling, gorgeous animal in heat. I am then the woman I always hoped I could be, and I love her.

While looking and feeling sexy is important in choosing party attire, submissives have yet another consideration: Easy removal! When play is occurring, submissives rarely stay dressed for long, and must therefore be somewhat more selective, choosing clothing where the areas of the body usually involved in play (such as the breasts, buttocks, thighs, genitals, etc.) can be easily uncovered. Often, with the exception (for women) of stockings and heels, the most flexible clothing is no clothing at all!

For the last ten years, the San Francisco Bay Area SM community has held flea markets (bizarre bazaars!) several times a year, attended most often by several hundred people where all can share, sell, and trade clothing and SM equipment. These have become extremely popular as much for the opportunity to share fashion, equipment, and ideas as for the social gathering.

There are rules of etiquette and safety at SM functions, and they are understood by all and communicated clearly to newcomers. Those who do not follow these guidelines may be asked to leave.

One newcomer to the SM community explored her perception of these rules in a letter to a local SM newsletter, commenting, as one example, on the fact that most submissives wear leather or metal collars which designate their status:

> It seems that a collar isn't mere decoration that one can wear oneself, like a decorative necklace. Instead, it must be put on you and indicates a very specific relationship with the person who puts it on. Once you're wearing the collar, there are specific ways of relating to your master/mistress and to other people. These things seem to be generally understood and expected.
>
> Another thing that surprised me was the attitude toward disobedience by bottoms. I would have thought that occasional disobedience might be looked on in fun, as a clear consent to punishment. But I'm told that that's sometimes a serious "no-no," and that Tops who are disobeyed can get truly pissed off. Occasionally, though, disobedient bottoms are really in for it . . . which may be, of course, exactly what they had in mind! Lots of paradoxes.

Attendance at parties depends on its sponsors and location, of course, and guests number anywhere from twenty to eighty. "Group" play scenes usually involve two, three, or four people and may take place within the view of others. SM parties are a paradise for both exhibitionists and voyeurs.

Etiquette requires that ongoing scenes not be interrupted,* and those who enjoy watching scenes done in the open are cautioned to do so from a discreet distance. Because some enjoy parties but prefer not to play in full view, where possibly there are places set aside for these more private players, depending, of course, on the limitations of the facility.

---

*Except on the rare occasions when a safeword is used and appears to be ignored, at which point anyone nearby will step in and stop the scene to protect the submissive.

The sponsors of every SM party are always on the lookout for unsafe activities and will speak to those involved if there is any problem. For example, play involving sharp instruments or lighted candles (dripping candle wax from lit candles is a common activity) is frowned on as potentially dangerous in a crowded playroom; such activities are best practiced privately.

Questions of safety and health are handled quickly and carefully because these matters take precedence over anything else, and most of us have made independent decisions with play partners as to what safety measures will be adopted and with whom. At most parties, condoms, individually packaged water-soluble lubricant, surgical gloves, and shower facilities are provided. The idea is to make the activities safe, easy, fun, and erotic. Indeed, many groups now sponsor safe-sex programs aimed at creative techniques to make the safety precautions erotic. There also is community controversy as to whether or not safe behaviors should be mandated at such functions, regardless of any individual arrangements.

As an example of the care taken to make parties problem-free, the following is an excerpt from a "handout" at a party:

> Welcome to our party! We've worked very hard to make this a comfortable space for the aficionado of safe and sane SM. Our motto is: "If there's no Safety and no Mutuality, then there's no SM."
>
> This is a place to have a good time, meet new friends and indulge in those secret fantasies you've always wanted to bring to light. To aid in this goal, we've come up with a few ideas and tips we'd like to pass along to you.
>
> [Some] CONSENSUALITY TIPS:
>
> DON'T BE PUSHY! Pushy people always get turned down.
>
> VOYEURISM is allowed at a respectful distance (ideally, they shouldn't even know you're there).
>
> DO NOT join or otherwise interrupt a scene in progress—and DO NOT barge into the scene to ask if you can be in it! This is just plan RUDE.
>
> CONFIDENTIALITY: People into SM are vilified by a number of groups and individuals, and many of us are "in the closet" as a result. We respect their right to privacy and request all party attendees to do the same. People who violate the privacy of others usually end up playing alone—and THAT's no fun at all!
>
> BEFORE YOU TRY a new piece of equipment, find out how to use it safely. There is always someone here you can ask.

SM etiquette does not usually include indiscriminate intermixing of partners and most often, the dominant's permission is required should someone want to play with a submissive, unless, of course, the submissive is attending without a partner. This arrangement allows the participants to decide with whom they will play and negotiate what kind of activities will go on within their scene.

From our party organizers:

> LIMITS should be carefully spelled out between partners. Discuss likes, fantasies, dislikes, and physical or emotional limitations. And remember: It's okay NOT to like something!

Just as casual SM encounters offer some specific things to the participants, group scenes or play in a public forum offer a different type of experience from what can be found in nonparty play. There is a sharing and learning of techniques that comes from playing or watching others play in the presence of others. Most of us love to talk about our play, and asking questions, appropriately timed, is both educational and fun. Often there is the advantage of introductions to new friends and lovers, as well as the garnering of group support. Sometimes, those of us who participate in SM parties do so specifically because the parties allow our exhibitionistic or voyeuristic proclivities free reign.

There are those who find a party atmosphere restrictive to their play. For instance, very intimate and intense play can be inhibited by the presence of others, and the concentration necessary for certain of the "trickier" activities (piercing, branding, hot wax, etc.) is more difficult to achieve in a crowded party atmosphere. Such activities are, therefore, often reserved for private times when the focus of the scene need not be on anything but the play and the players.

Interestingly enough, although SM is to many foreplay to sexual intercourse, it is rare to see intercourse in a party environment.

> I know it seems a weird distinction, but although I have no problem getting naked at a party and being whipped in front of 30 other people, I prefer to have sex in private. It just seems more intimate that way, and while I think it's okay to share SM play, sex to me is not a group affair. Besides, AIDS has made me sexually monogamous and so sex is something I share only with my husband.

SM AND SEX

In discussions about SM, a commonly asked question is "Sure, but do you still have *regular* sex?" referring specifically to sexual intercourse. It's a valid query and the answers are as diverse as the personalities and lives of the SMers themselves, but in almost all cases, the answer is YES.

According to the SM community, the main difference between "vanilla sex" and "SM sex" is an issue of sexual priorities. Where today's standards of sexual behavior would seem to clearly delineate foreplay and intercourse with orgasm as the only "acceptable activity," most of us believe our choice of sexual expression has broadened and redefined the parameters of "sex" to a level of sophistication in which neither intercourse nor orgasm are necessary, and where the goal of any such activity is sexual gratification.

> The variety of things we can do during a scene and the intensity of the energies being expended are so stimulating, so exciting, and so peacefully exhausting that nothing else could possibly enhance the feelings of total fulfillment and satisfaction. Most often, in fact, we're too tired after three or four hours of playing to even think about doing anything else!

Indeed, some believe that because SM offers such extremes of sexual intensity, excitement, and intimacy, vanilla sex in and of itself is not nearly as fulfilling as some combination of both.

> There's really no such thing as vanilla sex as long as my partners are part of my SM life. While we sometimes do engage in "regular" intercourse, in my mind there's always the possibility that some SM could creep into what we're doing. And so to me that is not vanilla sex. Even if nothing actively SM happens, my fantasies during sex are always SM in nature. So, again, I rarely view these activities as strictly vanilla.

▾   ▾   ▾

> Most of the time vanilla sex is not exciting for me. My erotic life is so full that it doesn't bother me at all that I'm not interested in vanilla sex. I think I'm doing a more sophisticated kind of sex— and anyway, intercourse is often part of our scene, so it's not like I never have intercourse. There's just more to it.

▾   ▾   ▾

> SM doesn't have to be genitally sexual, but the context of the play is still erotic and, of course, there's psychology involved, too. There's just something more going on in SM than in vanilla sex. It's an emotional, psychological release, and it's much more than "just plain sex."

▼   ▼   ▼

Is SM better than vanilla sex? Yes. Intercourse is a great part of it, sure, but it's so much more than that.

▼   ▼   ▼

As a woman, if I'm not playing with my lover, I actually prefer to do SM with gay guys. This removes any pressure towards intercourse along with the set of expectations that often accompany it, and the focus is on the experience, not on a sexual goal of intercourse or orgasm.

▼   ▼   ▼

My goal is SM intensity and when intercourse itself is not an issue, the freedom from "performance pressure" and sexual expectations allows us to concentrate fully on our SM communication and to direct our erotic energies in more diverse directions.

Despite these comparisons, intercourse often plays a part in sado-masochistic activity, but its integration into SM play, according to SMers, converts it from vanilla sex to SM sex. For example, the fantasy scene may see the mistress using her male "slave" as a sex object, a "stud," and as such, he will have intercourse with her to fulfill her sexual desires. In male dominant/female submissive play, intercourse might be integrated into an enactment of a slave or "kidnap/rape" fantasy.

These and a myriad of other creative uses integrates intercourse into SM play. In addition, vanilla sex often serves as the prelude to a scene or as an intimate rejoining of the partners after the separation their SM roles have perpetuated during play for some, while for others, SM is merely foreplay with intercourse the desired result. Often, however, intercourse is virtually impossible for the partners. Having spent anywhere from two to five hours in intense and emotionally draining SM play, the energy needed is simply not there.

The broader definition of sex in SM also works to avoid many of the problems associated with any sexual activity where the main goal is orgasm. Almost every sexually active person has experienced or been exposed, through movies, books, television, or friends, to sexual problems associated with the achievement, timing, or even lack of orgasm. The reasons are endless, encompassing everything from physical or psychological difficulties to drugs. But to the SM community, in many ways SM play without the need for orgasm can be likened to tantric sexuality.

> SM is more than just sex. It's an exchange of power, of dominance and submission. The submissive person gives himself to me. It transcends sex; it's so much more all-encompassing. Many times I don't have a physical climax, although I do have what I call mental climaxes; ongoing and overwhelming feelings of excitement, release, heat, enjoyment, fireworks, explosions and all! It's enjoying what you're doing and knowing that the person you're doing it with is enjoying it as much as you are; a give and take situation. It's more than just a physical climax because it's not necessarily genitally oriented or even a specific physical response; and, where orgasmic sex is short-lived and goal-oriented, these broader feelings can last much longer.

On the other hand:

> Orgasm does play a part in our SM, but our strictest rule during play is that no one comes without permission. This makes it really challenging. Getting closer and closer, asking, then begging, occasionally even pleading—never being sure if permission will be given or not—is a pleasurable agony. Or is it an agonizing pleasure?

The significance of the above discussion is that the purpose and goal of sexual activity, however defined or practiced, is physical and emotional satisfaction, and whatever the technique, these goals are shared by those of us who practice sadomasochism.

THE ORGANIZED SM COMMUNITY

As has been pointed out, we sadomasochists all once believed that our "odd" fantasies and desires were ours and ours alone, that they were not and could not be understood or accepted by anyone else on earth. We felt isolated and alone.

As we matured and became braver, we ventured out in search of a place of our own and discovered that there were really others out there who not only understood our needs but shared them. On a personal level, such discovery is enlightening and empowering. On a social level, however, we are isolated from everyday social interactions by our commitment to the SM lifestyle. We need each other, and once found, the ties that bind us are strong and communal. As with every community, sexual or otherwise, there is a need for structure, and so we began to create our own through the formation of social organizations that give our community places to meet and friends with whom to share.

We have said much about the SM community network and its reasons for being. Let us now explore the principles and operation of organized SM groups in general and look briefly at some specific groups. Since we are most familiar with the Northern California SM community and because this area boasts a very wide variety of SM organizations, we focus on this region, with the notation that similar groups exist in most larger cities countrywide.

SM groups usually advertise for members in local sexually oriented newspapers and in those with a broader circulation that will accept such advertising; few "mainstream" newspapers will accept SM-oriented advertisements. Such ads most often appear in the "Personal" or "Sexuality" categories of the classifieds, usually accepted with the caveat that specific sexual activities are not mentioned. For that reason, the emphasis is most often on dominance and submission. Many who answer these ads are more interested, they will admit, in finding sex partners and view SM only as a conduit. And in fact, the persistence and patience required for entry and acceptance into the organized SM community—usually including introductory orientation-type meetings, attendance under close supervision and only if accompanied by another member as sponsor, etc.—will usually screen out those whose interest is not specifically SM.

The first and largest SM group in the country, The Eulenspiegel Society (TES) of New York, deserves mention for its pioneering courage. Born in 1971 as the Masochist's Liberation Front (MLF), its first enthusiastic members could be found picketing with signs saying "We demand the right to be beaten" and "There is no freedom without servitude!" Not surprisingly considering the times, even the underground newspapers in New York City would not print MLF's advertising, and so its organizers decided to change the name to something less obvious, and they chose the current name.

Eventually, TES began attracting both dominant and submissive members, and since that time, has been open to SM people of all sexual orientations and persuasions. A part of the TES creed clearly articulates its reason for being and, indeed, articulates the sentiments of most SM groups:

> Most of all, we extend to our sisters and brothers who may be, as we once were, isolated, repressed, and frustrated, the word that they are not alone, that a Society exists for them—Straight, Gay, and

Bisexual, all working together with understanding and warmth, against misunderstandings and stereotypes, for freedom and fulfillment.

In 1974, the *Society of Janus* was founded in San Francisco and, after TES, is the oldest and largest SM organization in the country, and there are occasions when TES and Janus cooperate with each other on a variety of projects.

Janus has a membership of almost five hundred with half being local to the San Francisco Bay Area and, like TES, functions as an "umbrella" group, open to men and women of all sexual and SM orientations: Tops, bottoms, gays, straights, bisexuals, lesbians, transvestites, transsexuals—all are welcome. For once again, the more people involved, the stronger the support network.

Orientation meetings are a prerequisite for membership in Janus as well as almost all SM organizations. Members of most local SM groups also belong to Janus, which hosts twice-monthly informational program meetings with topics ranging from discussions on the psychology of SM to "Ask the Doctor" seminars on health and safety issues to demonstrations of whipping techniques to the pros and cons of switching from submission to dominance and back again.

The cost of meetings for members is about five dollars and guests pay seven dollars. Janus, along with most other groups, also sponsors parties several times a year; attendance is restricted to members and guests of members. The cost is about ten dollars a person.

Janus publishes a monthly newsletter called *Growing Pains* that contains fantasies, features, general information, personal ads and schedules of SM community events. Dues are forty dollars a year.

Gemini is a heterosexual male dominant/female submissive group whose membership is composed mostly of couples. Started by a local man who had the courage to solicit membership from the heterosexual population where no outreach before that time had ever been made, its numbers were stronger than might have been expected.

Now, while many Gemini members explore both roles in their private lives and/or belong to other organizations with different orientations, only male dominant/female submissive play is permitted at Gemini functions. Parties are held monthly and usually begin with a short information or education program before the call is out: "Let the games begin!" Gemini membership totals about one hundred; dues are forty dollars a year with party attendance at ten dollars a person.

Parties are open to members, guests of members and potential members with dates. Singles may attend without partners only under the sponsorship and supervision of a member.

SMC (Service of Mankind or SM Church) is a female dominant group that sponsors occasional parties and some ritual quasi-religious services based on goddess worship. There is a "priestess" at the head of the group who leads the meetings and occasionally officiates at members' weddings where an SM theme is wanted; because the group is officially designated as a church, such marriages are valid. Dues are forty dollars a year for women and couples, and somewhat more for single men. Membership numbers about three hundred.

La Madrona ("The Mistress") is a female dominant organization (a subsidiary group to the SMC) that sponsors parties several times a year. All submissives (male or female) must attend under the sponsorship of a dominant woman. Membership numbers about forty; there is no membership fee, and party attendance is about ten dollars a person.

The 15 is a gay men's group which sponsors occasional play parties at privately owned SM meeting and play facilities.

The Outcasts is a women's SM support group unrestricted by sexual or play orientation which sponsors occasional parties. The Outcasts replaced Samois, the strictly lesbian group mentioned earlier. Today, the Outcast group has about fifty members, and membership is twenty-five dollars.

CONFIDENTIALITY

One of the most important concerns for those of us in the SM community is confidentiality.

> For many of us, "coming out" was quite a risk, and the potential emotional ramifications of self-disclosure can be compounded by the very real risk of exposure and the intangible risk of losing control over your privacy. What confidentiality means in a social context is the right to privacy, the right to choose with whom you will share intimate details of your lifestyle such as your sexual preferences, your phone number and sometimes even your real name.

▼   ▼   ▼

> Maintaining confidentiality is really important. It means not disclosing what you see or hear at any SM function with anyone who wasn't there and not revealing anything told to you in confidence. This

requires thought and assumes integrity, but it's necessary; there's a lot at stake.

Working together, we create a community and engage in a lifestyle based on trust. With that foundation, we can outrageously but safely act out our fantasies together without shame.

To safeguard confidentiality, virtually every organized SM group has an elected or volunteer governing body of some sort, and it is these people alone who control membership lists, phone numbers, etc. Many of us use pseudonyms in order to protect ourselves, and our true names may be known only by the groups' leaders. This is done so that if, at the last minute, a meeting has been canceled or a party location changed, there is a way to contact the members. Since there are some instances where even a husband or wife may not know of their spouse's participation in SM, such contact is, of necessity, very discreet.

Wanting contact with someone one has met through such a group, a common occurrence, is handled this way:

> If I were, for example, to meet someone at a group function in whom I am interested (let's call him Jim), but neglected to get his number at the time, a call to the group asking for Jim's number would not suffice, for to give out such information would violate confidentiality. The director of the group, however, will contact Jim on my behalf, and Jim will be told that I would like to get in touch with him. If Jim agrees, one of two things will happen: The director would call me and give me Jim's number, or Jim would be given my number and asked to call.

Although somewhat burdensome, the need for confidentiality is never taken lightly.

> I belong to an SM group and our membership is closely screened. All potential members are asked what they do for a living—not specifically, but generally, what kind of business they are in. I work in the computer field and several years ago an application for membership came to our group from someone else in the same field. The group's director called me and gave me just the applicant's first name and a little business information to see if I knew him. I did. Because I was a long-time member, I was given the opportunity to say that I would prefer he not be accepted for membership at that time. The truth of the matter is that, had we met at a party, he would have had as much to lose by seeing me as I would have in meeting him there. This is specifically why the SM community is so tight. I know that I would have felt VERY uncomfortable at a party if he were there and while

it was too bad that his opportunity to join the group was lost for a time, my reputation and position as a member of the business community was too important to jeopardize; my seniority in the SM community gave me that right.

11

SM, Politics, and the Law*

There will always be those passionately opposed to sadomasochism, viewing it as a frightening and dangerous set of behaviors. This negative picture is often created and reinforced by the news media's lurid and inaccurate portrayals of SM and its practitioners. These intricate webs of misinformation act to perpetuate the myths about SM, mislead the general public and set the stage for the persecution of SM-oriented people.

Most SM-identified people endure social and psychological isolation within a hostile and disapproving society.

> DEAR ABBY: My problem is so personal that I have not been able to tell anyone about it. I am a 29-year old unmarried man in the military. While growing up, my mother seldom spanked me—even when I deserved it. The children I grew up with received more spankings than I did—and I always thought I should have been spanked more than I was. Now that I am a grown man, this desire to be spanked is still on my mind.
>
> On one occasion, I thought of asking a young woman I was dating to spank me, but I didn't have the nerve. I've heard that there are places where a guy can go to get a spanking, but I can't find one where I'm stationed. Part of me says that although I would not enjoy the pain, I would feel a lot better if I were on the receiving end of a good spanking. Another part of me says the whole thing is off the wall, and I should forget it.

---

*This chapter was written and edited by JJ Madeson, and the use of the term *we* is meant to indicate that she is speaking as a member of the SM community.

Abby, are there other men who want to be spanked by women? And what do you recommend for this problem?

Signed: Wants to Be Spanked

DEAR "WANTS": My psychiatric expert tells me that the desire to be spanked is a form of sadomasochism that is often linked with feelings of severe guilt—usually about sexuality. You say you always thought you should have been punished more than you were, strongly suggesting unconscious guilt. A professional therapist can help you understand the source of your guilt, and hopefully resolve it so you will no longer feel the need to be spanked. (You are attacking your problem from the wrong end.)[1]

It is not surprising that Dear Abby's "psychiatric expert" claims that sadomasochism is "often linked with feelings of severe guilt" since SM is still defined by the psychological and health-care community as a category of mental illness. Indeed, until recently, even homosexuality was defined as an illness. Only after a great deal of lobbying and extensive research was it reclassified, recognizing at last that gays and lesbians were no more neurotic than any other segment of the population.

So even "Dear Abby" has once again validated the belief that SM desires are abnormal and should be "resolved [read: ignored or repressed] so you will no longer feel the need to be spanked."

The SM community had a different response:

Abby, this man's letter talked about his need to be spanked, while your response talked about guilt and punishment. The only "guilt" I saw in his letter was a healthy anxiety about being himself in our rather judgmental culture. One way the world can make progress is by learning to respect people who are different.

Sometimes the repression is more tangibly damaging, such as the loss of a job. At its worst, however, anti-SM sentiment can go to horrible extremes. Like all minorities, people who practice SM make easy targets for those with political, religious, or legal agendas.

When practiced by consenting adults, SM as a sexual practice is not, per se, illegal, but that does not deter zealous public officials from putting consenting adults in prison.

SM activity has sometimes been prosecuted under felony assault laws, situations in which the state itself presses criminal charges even without a complaint from—and often over the strong objections of—the alleged "victim." This is the precise situation in the ongoing Spanner case, recently prosecuted in Great Britain. Several gay men (Tony Brown, Roland Jaggard, and the late Colin Laskey) were arrested during their SM play, the Top being charged with assault. Despite the protestations of the submissive man that these were consensual activities, he, too, was charged—with conspiracy to commit assault!

This case, and several others tested whether consent to sexual activity is a valid defense against such charges. As late as May 1995, in the English Crown Court, a defendant (Alan Wilson) was convicted of "assault occasioning actual bodily harm." His "crime" had been to brand his initials on his wife's buttocks using a hot knife, *at her request.* The judge in this case directed the jury that they were bound to convict, and ruled recently that "the satisfaction of a sadomasochistic libido" did not provide for consent as a valid defense against a charge of bodily harm.

In fact, the Wilson conviction noted above was appealed, and the English appeals court has recently declared that "sexual activity between husband and wife in the privacy of the home is not a matter for criminal investigation, let alone criminal prosecution. The court further said that the proceedings should never have been brought and "had served no useful purpose."

It is hoped that the European Court of Human Rights to which the Spanner defendants have appealed will see fit later this year to follow the intelligent reasoning of the reviewing court in the Wilson case and acquit the defendants.

Another such case took place in the 1980s in Massachusetts when a man was sentenced to ten years in prison for hitting his lover lightly with a riding crop in the context of a consensual SM Experience.

It could happen that an SM couple is making love. Police, perhaps called by neighbors alarmed by the noise, or perhaps looking for an excuse to arrest one of the parties, break in on the scene. They arrest the Top and charge her with assault. The Bottom could protest all the while that they were only making love, but their partner is still hauled off to jail.

If the couple is gay or unmarried, the submissive could even be subpoenaed and forced to testify against their partner in court. While the protests of the Bottom might not save the Top from prison, they might be used as evidence to declare the Bottom mentally incompetent. Again, only the distortions of anti-SM bigotry could locate the abuse of power in this scenario within the SM relationship rather than with outsiders who interfere with it.[2]

The legal vulnerability of SM was earlier demonstrated by a string of police actions in Canada, when Toronto police raided a local gay SM bathhouse. They charged several men under the Bawdy House Laws ("a place resorted to for purposes of prostitution or lewdness") and confiscated all SM sex toys, including dildoes, leather harnesses, whips, and so on. Although Bawdy House Laws were intended as anti-prostitution measures, no prostitution was ever alleged in this case.

The law contained, however, a vague phrase referring to a "place where indecent acts take place," and the police argued that SM sex is indecent and any place where it occurs is a bawdy house. While this interpretation has not been clearly upheld in court, the arrests and trials continued.

Needless to say, press coverage in this raid was overtly sensational, picturing the confiscated SM equipment in great detail. The gay community in Toronto protested the raid, the nature of the charges, and the press coverage; with help from other SM communities, they also raised the funds to cover the substantial cost of the legal defense.

Sadly, most people prosecuted in the United States for nontraditional sexual behavior are not so lucky. Attempts to repress such behavior is not surprising when it comes from the conservative far right or from opportunistic politicians. In the past decade, however, an attack on SM has been mounted from a most unexpected direction: the mainstream feminist movement, particularly the radical lesbian faction.

In the mid-1980s, a book called *Against Sadomasochism* was published by a group of women calling themselves "radical feminists,"* which clearly articulated the vast philosophical differences between the women who practice SM and those women who believe both sadomasochism itself and its practitioners to be morally corrupt.

> Many members of the women's community, as outsiders, see only the hurting in the SM experience, never the touching of the fine line between pleasure and pain to heighten pleasure. They see the acting out of power, never the demonstration of consensuality. They see the pain or humiliation, never the sharing, concern, love.
>
> Yet, all of these aspects are part of the SM experience; they just are not part of the stereotypes by which the experience is judged.[3]

For the most part, the editors of *Against Sadomasochism* were self-described lesbian feminists—as were, surprisingly, those the book

---

*This and other such terms used in this section are meant only to describe the women of the anti-SM movement; we do not mean to include feminists, radicals, lesbians,

indicted most stridently for their enjoyment of sadomasochistic sexuality.

> SM is not the sharing of power; it is merely a depressing replay of the old and destructive dominant/subordinate mode of human relations and one-sided power, which is even now grinding our earth and our human consciousness into dust.[4]

Against Sadomasochism not only targeted SM lesbians but also broadly attacked, in a myriad of ways, all women who enjoy SM sexuality:

> ... women have always been subjugated to the power of a male dominated society, and [we] suggest that any woman, whether heterosexual, homosexual or bisexual, who participates in sadomasochism ... is reinforcing the form of that hierarchy.[5]

At the time of the publication of *Against Sadomasochism*, this radical lesbian feminist viewpoint began appearing in feminist events of all types.

In 1986, a symposium was held at Mount Holyoke College entitled "Feminism, Sexuality, and Power," attended by Margaret Hunt, a pro-SM feminist and contributor to Samois' second book, *Coming to Power*. Among the issues discussed at the symposium was "convincing currently heterosexual women to stop participating in their own oppression by continuing to have sex and/or orgasms with men."[6]

"The main problem with this view," suggests Ms. Hunt, "is the exaggerated emphasis that it places on sex acts in explaining women's oppression."[7]

In her essay "The Elect Clash with the Perverse," Ms. Hunt explored this astounding premise:

> Feminist cosmology not only equates all or almost all heterosexuality, even between two consenting adults, with rape (the assumption being that women are being coerced into it even when they think they are doing it of their own free will) but tends to see heterosexuality (i.e., rape) pervading the whole of reality. All the world's a stage, according to this view, on which is being enacted a kind of gigantic cosmic rape scene. There is a never-ending dialectic between heterosexuality and all other oppressive acts in society: the bedroom de-

---

or otherwise (however they classify themselves) who are open to the idea of freedom of sexual choice.

fines, legitimates and perpetuates "hetero-patriarchy" in a horrifying cycle of sick fantasy, rape, violence and victimization.[8]

Against Sadomasochism continues, that

> while paying lip service to consensual sex, the sexual revolution ignores the power systems which create inequality and make meaningful consent an impossibility ... and so all this bullshit about consensual sex, changing roles back and forth, safewords, etc. ad nauseam—is, to my mind, just a cover that encourages women to be violent. Sadomasochism is violence.[9]

Thus, the bewigged lords of the British court and the intolerant of the radical feminist movement pass judgment on sadomasochism on the same intolerant and intolerable grounds: we sadomasochists are crazy or deluded or otherwise incapable of deciding what's best for ourselves.

The objections from women who enjoy SM, heterosexual and lesbian, are loud and clear:

> The consensual fantasies in which I indulge in the privacy of my playroom or bedroom have nothing at all to do with whether or not women have been or are victimized sexually by men or by anyone else. To think otherwise is ridiculous.

▼ ▼ ▼

> It is an unfortunate habit of sexual thought that people so readily assume that something they would not like would be equally unpleasant to someone else. For example, I hate to run. I might someday change my mind, but at this point, it would take a lot of coercion to get me to run around the block, let alone for five miles. This does not mean that my friends who run in marathons are sick, brainwashed, or [do so] at gunpoint.[10]

▼ ▼ ▼

> The idea that there is an automatic correspondence between sexual preferences and political beliefs is long overdue to be jettisoned.[11]

▼ ▼ ▼

> I believe those with the inclination and courage to explore realms of pain, power and sexuality should be free to do so. Power is not an invention of men, to be wished out of existence in a new women's society. Power is the capacity to make things happen—power is energy—and we would do well to know as much as we can about it.[12]

The liberating power of conscious and consensual SM play has, in fact, been one of the major forces in the formation of the lesbian women's movement. Samois, the first organization specifically for lesbian SM, has been a strong and articulate voice for both lesbian and SM communities nationwide. This organization was a coming of age for these women—and for many since then; an acknowledgement and acceptance that despite differences in opinion among its members, there was a need to stand together with the integrity of their SM experience.

The rest of the SM community, with Samois' help and guidance, have made great strides since that time to free its women and those in the general public from the attitudes that would blithely condemn our behavior. I would like to believe that this book will also help to reinforce the understanding of SM as a sexual *choice* (emphasis on "choice") that we make with our eyes open.

Another position of these radical women (which applies equally to their opposition to sadomasochistic sex and to heterosexuality in general) states that women who participate in any sexual act by and with men only do so only by way of social coercion.

> They're kidding, right? Isn't it preposterous (not to mention just plain silly) to believe that when someone (in this case, a woman) consents—voluntarily agrees—to do something, they do so only because they have been coerced into that agreement? Sorry. I don't buy it.

Consensuality (the basic premise of the SM lifestyle), according to these women, does not even exist. This position is almost too preposterous to contemplate seriously.

> These feminists are incredible. They're like communists. They decide what's natural and what's right and wrong, and they expect us all to live by it.[13]

This issue of consent, as we have seen, is one that significantly affects the SM community and its practices. Since there is simply no doubt whatever in any of our minds that our sexual behavior is consensual, informed and valid, this ignorant attitude goes to the value of our freedom to choose—allegedly the very foundation of the women's movement.

Intolerance and political rhetoric seem to be the foundations upon which these radicals build their arguments against the moral and sexual corruption of sadomasochistic activities, but the romance of revolution has convoluted their perceptions of healthy sexuality. Their rhetoric speaks of violence and oppression in SM sexuality where neither exist; their intolerance seems naively misplaced in a women's movement based upon choice.

> Repression in the guise of protection? Interesting concept. But we are not fooled by this sheep in wolf's clothing. They may allege they're just trying to help us poor misguided women, but repression is repression, and it is unacceptable.

▼ ▼ ▼

> As long as outsiders leave us alone, we have no quarrel with them. The only conflict comes from nosey people trying to impose their values on others—not the other way around.[14]

The sadomasochistic lifestyle, as we have said all along, can be potentially dangerous, but with safe, sane and consensual attitudes and behavior, those of us who practice it are willing to take what we knowledgeably consider to be minimal risks. In the end, then, the response to the women of *Against Sadomasochism* and others is: "If you haven't taken the risks, you don't get to make the rules."[15]

12

The Downside
of the Dark Side*

As with any interest, sport, hobby, passion, or pursuit, there
are disadvantages, dangers, and downsides to the practice of sadomasochism. Something can always go wrong, and it is to the benefit of
those involved to make themselves aware of the possibilities and to
be prepared to deal with any situation that may arise. Before perishing
in Antarctica, Admiral Scott wrote in his journal: "I do not regret this
journey; we took risks, we knew we took them, things have come out
against us, therefore we have no cause for complaint."

There are several distinct categories into which such considerations
can fall, and chief among them are the physical, the emotional and the
social aspects of our chosen lifestyle.

Let us first consider the physical elements of an SM lifestyle. Let us
say once again that the real SM horror stories are few. Sadomasochism is
sophisticated sex play making use of potentially dangerous equipment
and complex mind games, where the line between fantasy and reality
can become blurred, true, but while we know of no one who has been
seriously or permanently injured through SM activities, SM has been
with us for centuries, and it is likely that there have been such
occurrences.

> Injuries and accidents do occur in the course of sexual activity and
> SM is not exempt. But by and large, SM, particularly when practiced
> by people in touch with SM communities, has a safety record most
> sports teams would envy.[1]

---

*This chapter was written and edited by JJ Madeson, and the use of the term *we* is
meant to indicate that she is speaking as a member of the SM community.

The present day SM community's credo and practice of "safe, sane, sober, and consensual" behavior acts as protection against some of the physical dangers of SM play.

As any newspaper will reveal, there are always murders, kidnaps, rapes, and other crimes that seem to have an element of SM about them. Most often, though, the people to whom such news stories refer are seasoned criminals, psychopaths, sociopaths, and the like; they are certainly not the responsible sadomasochists we have been talking with and about in this book. Once again, the equation is simple: SM is consensual, violence is not; SM is not violence, nor is violence SM.

Usually, SM "horror stories" are simply scenes that really scared one or more of the participants, scenes in which something unexpected happened or went wrong. Most often this happens because the partners have not sufficiently communicated their needs, desires, or limitations.

I have always had fantasies about castration. [Authors' note: castration fantasies are very common among men; they are the equivalent in intensity to rape fantasies among women.] Since fantasy magazines often have ads from other men with similar fantasies looking for "sexual penpals," I often correspond with these men just for fun. At one point, I had quite a letter fantasy going with one man, and he often mentioned an organization with which he was familiar that allegedly acted out men's castration fantasies (this was long before Lorena Bobbitt!). I even corresponded with members of the organization until I began to suspect that they were interested in more than fantasy. They alluded to the performance of actual castration rituals. I can't prove it, of course—fantasy being fantasy—but the suspicion was enough. I broke off the correspondence as soon as I realized the problem. I knew that my fantasy, however real it might sometimes have seemed, WAS a fantasy, and while I still enjoy such fantasies, I'm really, really clear that I want no part of the real thing.

▼　▼　▼

Four of us were playing out a fantasy together, and the scenario was that Sam and I were the bad guys. Blake and Marilyn had returned from the movies, and we had surprised them when they got home. We grabbed them, blindfolded them, threatened them and began to remove their clothes. Blake was on his hands and knees in front of me, and I was cutting his pants off with a very small, sharp paring knife. I had the knife under the waistband of his slacks and was sawing through it, pulling the knife straight towards me. On the way up, the knife point went right into the underside of my arm. It didn't hurt and didn't bleed right away so I continued playing. After a few minutes more, though, I noticed it was bleeding. Without breaking the scene, I went to the bathroom to wash the cut. I put a bandaid over it (it was that small a cut) and by the time I got back downstairs, the bandaid was soaked with blood. I obviously needed more than a bandaid so I stopped the scene and asked for some help. Blake is a physician so he was able, with pressure and a heavier bandage, to stop the bleeding. I was pretty frightened by this time, although the cut itself wasn't hurting.

We spent the rest of the evening socializing rather than playing, and the next morning, we went to the emergency room for a tetanus shot and a clean dressing. It was a stupid mistake but, thank goodness, not a costly one.

There are some SM activities which are more dangerous than others. Such edge-play activities (on the edge of and closest to danger), including almost all uses of knives and needles, electricity, long-term bondage and breath control play are safe *only* in the hands of highly experienced, sane and sober sadomasochists who know what to do should something go wrong. In fact, many of us believe that some of these activities should not be done at all.

Another physical danger is the long-term possibility of disease, from venereal conditions to hepatitis to AIDS. The SM community nation-wide has lost many of its valued members to the consequences of disease, and while there is enough knowledge to combat such risks, there is also no such thing as too safe.

These are some of the physical considerations that limit us in our SM activities, but being aware of these and similar things and taking the responsibility seriously helps us avoid any real crises—medical or otherwise.

Another consideration is the very real possibility of playing with someone who is either totally inexperienced or who feels that they know more than they do. Such gaps in knowledge can prove dangerous. Most often, such situations are easily handled by not playing with an unfamiliar partner unless there are others around; there is safety in numbers.

Psychologically and emotionally, some play can be wrenching. Humiliation, fear, and the fine line between fantasy and reality could conceivably weaken or damage one's mental health. As examples, here are the enactment of interrogation, or Spanish Inquisition themes, where the danger—even between lovers—is the potential for serious mental breaks caused by very intense play upon the mind of a fragile or unstable individual. This may be a major reason that most SMers we have encountered are relatively stable people; they are very in touch with their own egos, needs, desires, and limitations. Practicing SM successfully, mentally and physically, requires "together," knowledgeable people. We want to say again that SM is an art—for most a studied, practiced lifestyle—and should not be tried by those who do not know what they are doing.

> When we started to play, he began by asking me a question: Why are you here? I tried as many answers as I could: Because I want to be; because it's fun; because I love you; because you want me to be here. Each answer brought only punishment, and the harsher and harsher that punishment became, the more and more confused I got. And still the question continued: Why are you here? Why are you here? Why are you here? At some point, I broke. I cried, I yelled, I got mad, I protested, I begged him to tell me the answer he wanted. He only repeated the question.
>
> About an hour into this, I no longer knew how to handle this type of interrogation scene, and I said the only thing left to me: "Red." I didn't want to say it—hated saying it, in fact—but I had to stop the confusion going on in my mind. After all, I thought this was a "game."
>
> When the questioning finally stopped, I cried with relief and said the only words left to my confused brain: I want to go home. So I did.
>
> In the next several days, we talked about the experience, and I realized that I had not been prepared to deal with the amorphous scenario where his part was understood and mine was not. It was too intense and illogical for me, and my only response was to end it. Basically, what we had was a "failure to communicate."

For some, SM can become dangerously all-encompassing, an obsession. As with any obsession, one then loses the possibility of choice. Freedom is the ability to make a choice, and that is what SM is about: being free to make a choice about one's personal and sexual self-expression.

Some of us, especially as novices, worry that our attraction to this lifestyle will become an addiction, necessitating escalating levels of more dangerous play. Experience teaches, however, that this fear is usually groundless. Indeed, each play experience (whether with a new playmate or an "old" partner) is so different from the one before, even if no new activities are done, that it always *seems* new and exciting.

If our SM life becomes so all-encompassing that we neglect our responsibilities, its importance is, of necessity, forced into narrower parts of our lives, and we have to learn moderation to keep the SM in perspective.

Each time I play with someone, it is a totally new experience. Even if we do the same things we've done for years, it always seems different, and so the "I'm-bored-with-this, let's-try-something-heavier" scenario rarely occurs. Even when I play with someone I've played with many times before—even if we were to do tonight exactly what we did last night—it *feels* like something we've never done before because the moods, the attitudes, the music, the lighting, the company—all are never just the same again.

▼ ▼ ▼

She asked me once: Don't you get used to the pain, the intensity, the high you get from playing? The true answer is "never." The variety of what we do is limited only by our wildest imagination, and I don't see how I could ever be bored. It's as simple as that.

There are other risks here as well, such as the possibility of beginning an SM relationship with someone who turns out to be dangerous or psychopathic, or both.

On those very few occasions many years ago when I played alone with someone new, I realized midway through the scene that I really had no idea who this person really was, what his motivations or predilections or background might be. Over the years, these risks have seemed enormous and as I have matured into my SM lifestyle, I no longer allow myself solitary play with a new person. I make sure there are always others around. It's the only safe thing to do.

Another emotional issue for many of us is that, with the intensity of SM and the incredible intimacy between partners that such play engenders, there is a risk—maybe a better word is "likelihood"—of quickly falling in love with someone who is really just a friend or a play partner. The speed with which such attachments can form can be detrimental to the play relationship, especially in cases where there was never an intent to form any such deep commitment.

The first time I met Phil, we talked for hours since he was a novice and was trying to prepare for his first party. We had a really good level of communication, and by the time we got to the party, we were getting along really well. About halfway through the party, he came up to me in a quiet moment and asked me to marry him! I had to tell him that he was in love with this new world he had discovered and not with me, but that I appreciated the sentiments. I know that starting out in SM can bring on some pretty strong emotions, but that's the first time I got a marriage proposal out of it!

In addition, those who have attempted to live out their SM roles twenty-four hours a day, seven days a week, have found that their relationship under these circumstances suffers, and the trade-off is not positive.

Constant playing, too, can be self-defeating.

> My mind really wants to just play and play and play and never stop, but my body knows better, and I always poop out sooner than I want to. I suppose it's possible just to play for days without stopping, but since I need to be able to walk and eat and go to work, I do have to curb my desires. I hate that, but it's a fact of life.

▼ ▼ ▼

> I was a pro-dom [professional dominatrix] for several years and discovered that having all the responsibility to do the work of a scene five or six times a day was just too much. Not only was I too tired to give my best energies to my husband, I had very little interest in playing at all; it was too much a business. So I stopped the professional work and went back to my "regular" kinky life.

The longest list of downside elements to an SM lifestyle can be found in the category of "social" ramifications.

The first and most important here is probably the secrecy of it all.

> Most of my difficulties relating to my involvement in SM have been leaving family and friends in the dark. There are very good reasons why this has been necessary, but it does make them wonder about my busy social life. When I say I'm going out for the night or that I have something planned for the evening, the questions inevitably begin: Where are you going? Why can't I come along? Inquiring minds may want to know, but I can't always tell them.

▼ ▼ ▼

> While I can think of mostly positive impacts SM has had on my personal life, there is a negative aspect of the lifestyle that comes to mind when SM people are viewed as a community. Specifically, the issue is the invisibility and fear of us and our activities by society. The degree to which SM is misunderstood, considered bizarre, sick, and dangerous by society at large, makes it necessary for most of us to be silent about our sexuality. It seems ludicrous to those of us involved in SM that something that is fun, consensual, pleasurable, and draws people together in such a positive way should receive such condemnation. SM is an activity that affirms what it means to be fully human in all its complexity and creativity but one that remains invisible because of the ignorance about what it really is.

Indeed, we sadomasochists have found something that makes us feel wonderful, yet there are few with whom we can fully share our happiness. Had we taken up painting or sculpture or writing or athletics as a recreational activity, there would be no reason to hide it.

> But I have chosen to make SM a major part of my recreation, and that means I also have to live with the consequences of my choice. I know that, but even paranoids have real enemies, and my paranoia has wide impacts that have shaped my life. I feel I need to have a separate mailing address and a phone message service which take both time and money to maintain; many of my acquaintances in the community don't even know my real name, but these protections seem necessary if I am to maintain the separateness of my two lives, which I feel I must do. Most people involved in either my "regular" or my "kinky" lifestyle know nothing of those on the "other side."

This is significant because SM is more than just a subject that we cannot talk about; it often means business associates and/or family cannot easily be introduced to our SM friends (who are often, by the way, our only friends); it means further that we are hesitant to let any of our friends from the SM community into our vanilla world.

> It is like I'm caught in a science fiction drama, a hero who occasionally slips between dimensions in search of adventure, but it means that the hero is often alone since no one from either dimension may know the other and the hero cannot be truly intimate with anyone.

Thus, having found a niche in life, a place where we truly belong, that knowledge must often be ours alone.

It is often both risky and scary for the singles in the SM community to date and introduce straight men or women to the topic, so if the wish is to continue their SM lifestyle, there are limitations on who they are comfortable dating.

Indeed, opening the subject up with those we would like to involve in our world can be a daunting task, one that often leads to the disappearance from our lives of those same people. The same is true even for family members.

> I've been in the scene for fifteen years. It is almost all of my social life and one hundred percent of my sexuality. Although my family is not local, they do come to visit and not one of them knows where my interests lie. It's not that I'd willingly share my sexual interests

with my family, but my whole social involvement with this community must remain a deep secret.

For me personally, one of my sisters is in the publishing business,
and as desperately as I would wish to share the existence of this book
and its significance in my life, it is a joy I must keep to myself. I know
that if the subject matter were almost anything other than what it is,
she would be proud of me for having written a book. I'd very much
like to have her share my pride and sense of accomplishment, but on
this one, I stand necessarily mute. I would wish it to be otherwise.
But I cherish our friendship, and I believe this knowledge could truly
destroy it. I think that's very sad.

Sometimes, SM can cause problems within a relationship:

> The man I was dating was a VERY GOOD dominant. Our SM play was
> exceptional; he was one of the best Tops I had ever played with. After
> a while, I noticed that, because he *was* such a strong Top, I expected
> him to be dominant and in control of all aspects of our relationship.
> He was not able to do that, and indeed, I was asking too much. I had
> to learn to differentiate clearly our SM/sex relationship as separate
> from our "other" lives. I needed to take responsibility for myself at
> times other than during SM play, and my expectations really put a
> strain on our relationship.

From the professional side of sadomasochism comes some further
elements of the downside, one of which relates again to the need for
secrecy and society's refusal to accept the provision of such services
as a viable profession.

> Despite the recent ruling by a New York court that professional
> dominance did not constitute prostitution, would-be dominatrices
> will not find government and business agencies accepting of their
> profession. Whether applying for a business license . . . setting up a
> commercial bank account, applying to process credit cards, or even
> just paying taxes, the professional often hears, "Oh, no, we can't say
> *that*. Let's just say you're an actress or a tutor or a therapist or
> whatever." Anything but what you really are.
>
> So while those of us who are trying to operate within the system
> pay all the attendant costs, we find that we still have not reaped the
> benefits of the system's protections, and we are forced into fraud at
> every step.

Another experienced SMer notes:

> It's like being a teacher in a tough inner-city school. You have to get
> past the sleaze, the users, the crime, the drugs, and all that other

crap, to try to reach that one person out there who is really going to appreciate the time and effort that you have put into developing your craft, and with whom you can share that crazy, wonderful roller-coaster ride, which is truly what great SM sessions feel like.

Then there are the clients who attempt (unsafely) to reproduce at home the experiences they have had in their sessions with the professional, undermining all of the efforts made by those who care about education and safety issues in the practice of SM arts.

> I get a call from the hospital from a guy that I've spent months trying to train into the safe application of these techniques, but who decided to try a session with a cute novice kid who had decided that putting on a leather miniskirt and buying a cheap riding crop made her a Mistress, who suddenly believed she knew all the subtleties of stringent rope bondage. Except for the part about not cutting off nerve pathways or major arterial blood flow. She forgot about that.

For elected officials, public figures and others in high-profile positions, participation in an SM lifestyle and the potential for discovery poses far more significant risks than it does for ordinary sadomasochists. Careers, public favor or position are at stake, and for such people, any time spent on establishing and maintaining the secrecy of their private lives is well worth the effort.

There is one other interesting downside for those of us, especially women, who practice SM, and that is the legal dilemma in which we would find ourselves should we become a true victim of an attack, an assault, a rape, or a beating. Should such a thing take place, it might prove difficult to bring and maintain such a charge against the offender once any investigation began to reveal our lifestyle. Wouldn't it be tempting for an attorney or a jury to doubt the validity of such a claim, saying, "Well, she does that kind of thing every weekend with her friends. Why is this any different?" It *is* different, of course, but it would have to be a consideration for any sadomasochist and their lawyer should such an incident take place.

> And then sometimes, things just go wrong. . . . A little while back, I was fooling around with a pair of handcuffs someone had left behind after a party when I accidentally locked one of them around a wrist (I know, I know, pretty stupid!). When I began to look for the key (something I obviously should have done *first!*), it was nowhere to be found. So there I sat, thinking, "Swell. Now what?" I called the friends I know that have the largest toy collection, and they said

"Come on over. We have plenty of keys to try." It turned out, after trying several keys, we were able to open the cuff. But what if they hadn't been home, then what? I couldn't—wouldn't—have asked a cop; there would just be too many questions. The consensus, as I talked about it with friends, was that I could have gone to a locksmith. I'm not sure I *ever* would have thought of that myself, but at least I'll know for next time!

▼ ▼ ▼

I was working for a law firm and had to make a delivery of some papers to City Hall. The weekend before, my Top had fastened a thin silver chain around my waist with a decorative padlock. It was a symbolic, private gesture between us, but when the chain set off the metal detectors at City Hall, it comes as no surprise that I was at a loss for what to say! I mumbled around for a little, trying to figure out how to explain the problem. Finally, figuring that nothing is too wierd in San Francisco, I just told him I was wearing a chain around my waist. I offered to show him. To my surprise, he said with some embarrassment, "Oh, OK. Go ahead." Whew!

▼ ▼ ▼

I had just dropped my wife off to catch a train and had set our home security alarm when we left. Apparently, though, I had hit the wrong button and set off the alarm. I did not realize it, of course, until I came home to find two police cars in my driveway, lights flashing. There were two cops coming out of my house, guns drawn. We all met halfway down the driveway, and we were able to figure out what had happened with the alarm. They said the house appeared to be okay and they left. I went inside and suddenly remembered that we had played the night before, the playroom was wide open, toys all over the floor. I was *so* embarrassed, wondering what on earth the cops must have thought! None of the stuff is illegal really, just supremely embarrassing.

So there are disadvantages, there is a downside to an SM lifestyle. We hope, though, that we have all been able to learn to juggle these elements of our lifestyle so that our experiences are, for the most part, positive. We learn to look out for ourselves and our friends, recognize potential dangers and do what we can to avoid them before they become real problems. If and when something does go wrong, we know that honesty—not secrecy, difficult though it may be—must prevail when we talk to doctors, lawyers, police or others to whom we turn for help.

We understand also that we must, to the best of our abilities, keep our sense of humor. These are simply games we are playing; we are doing it for fun; and we do not want the consequences to outweigh the benefits.

Odds and Ends

SM play is not without humor and that's an important thing to remember when things go wrong. I was being very dominant once and accidentally tripped over a bondage rope and ended up almost standing on my submissive's hand. The only thing I could think of to say—dominantly, of course—was "I *meant* to do that, slut!"

▼ ▼ ▼

We go away for the weekend with one suitcase full of clothes and three bags full of toys—each one weighs a ton! We usually take many more toys than we actually use, but we want to be free to do just about anything. We most often travel with our toys in locked bags to keep away from prying eyes of hotel maids. We must also keep watch on our noise levels—curious next door neighbors or cops are not a fun idea. But then, no one ever said this weird lifestyle would be easy!

▼ ▼ ▼

SM is forgetting to take off your steel cockring, and it sets off the alarm at the airport!

▼ ▼ ▼

We were going to Jamaica for a week and had to get very creative with our packing. We didn't think whips and stuff were illegal, but discovery would sure be embarrassing. So . . . we threaded whips into pants' legs, riding crops on the bottom edge of the case and also hidden in slacks; metal nipple clamps were out, but clothespins were an easy substitute. Then we found the most bored-looking Customs agent who didn't even open the bags! It was really sort of scary but an exciting challenge.

▾ ▾ ▾

SM is tiny gold handcuff earrings with an elegant, expensive dress for the opera.

▾ ▾ ▾

SM is the quiet typist by day who becomes a whip-wielding dominatrix by night; or the submissive secretary who goes to work with a leather slave collar under her turtleneck sweater.

▾ ▾ ▾

SM is the secret thrill of wandering through a hardware store, buying fifty feet of heavy chain, and finding perverse private uses for ordinary things that would make the salesman blush—if he only knew!

▾ ▾ ▾

SM is trying to explain the massive eyebolts in your ceiling to your landlady who listens with flat eyes ... and you know your lease is ending.

▾ ▾ ▾

Dear Columnist: I'm about to buy my first black leather jacket, and I'm really excited. However, I want to make sure I buy the appropriate ones for parties and events. Is there a right and wrong kind of black leather jacket? Jerry the Novice.

Answer: Indeed there is, Jerry. Keep in mind that you'll be buying the jacket for the black leather itself—for the look and feel of the material, not for the thermal function of the garment. So don't make the mistake of buying a fashion leather jacket or a recreational leather jacket. Then you'd just be getting a *jacket* made of black leather instead of black *leather* in the form of a jacket. In other words, you don't want a leather-jacket *jacket*; you want a *leather* leather-jacket. To a novice, the two may look (and may even be) identical, but they can be easily distinguished by the way they are merchandized. Leather-jacket jackets are sold in regular clothing stores, while leather leather-jackets are sold in SM specialty stores. Therefore, don't go to a leather-store *store*; go to a *leather* leather-store. Unfortunately, this kind of marketing means that leather leather-jackets are inherently more expensive than leather-jacket jackets. Maybe you'd rather be saving money—but hey, the scene tops the players, if you know what I mean! If this whole situation is too overwhelming, you may just want to get something less expensive for now, like a hot-looking black leather belt. Of course, you don't want a leather-belt *belt*, you want a *leather*-leather-belt, so it's back to the leather-leather-store again.[1]

Notes

PREFACE

1. Larry Townsend, *Leathermen's Handbook II* (NY: Carlyle Communications, 1983), 19.

CHAPTER 1: DEFINITION

1. Gloria/William Brame, Jon Jacobs, *Different Loving* (NY: Villard Books, 1994), 17.
2. Samois, *Coming to Power* (Boston: Alyson Press, 1984), 31.
3. Havelock Ellis, *Studies in the Psychology of Sex*, Vol. 1, (Random House, NY; 1938) (originally published in 1901).
4. Townsend, *Leathermen's Handbook II*, 18.
5. Brame/Jacobs, *Different Loving*, 6.
6. Geoff Mains, *Urban Aboriginals: A Celebration of Leathersexuality* (San Francisco: Gay Sunshine, 1984), 100.
7. Brame/Jacobs, *Different Loving*, 47.
8. Philip Miller/Molly Devon, *Screw the Roses, Send Me the Thorns* (Fairfield, CT: Mystic Rose Books, 1995), 3.
9. Gini Graham Scott, *Dominant Women, Submissive Men* (NY: Praeger Publishers, 1983; republished as *Erotic Power*, NJ: Citadel, 1984), xii.
10. Miller/Devon, *Screw the Roses, Send Me the Thorns*, 20.
11. *Id.* at 21.
12. Ellis, *Studies in the Psychology of Sex*, Vol. 1.
13. Weinberg/Williams/Moser, *The Social Constituents of Sadomasochism*, Social Problems, Vol. 31, April 1984
14. Mains, *Urban Aboriginals*, 29.

CHAPTER 2: WHAT DO WE KNOW ABOUT SADOMASOCHISM?

1. Brame/Jacobs, *Different Loving*, 20.
2. Reik, Theodor, *Masochism & Modern Man* (Farrar & Rinehart, NY; 1941).
3. C. S. Ford & Beach, F.A., *Patterns of Sexual Behavior* (Herpet & Brothers, Scranton, PA; 1981).
4. Baumeister, Roy F., *Masochism & The Self*, (Lawrence Erlbaum Associates, NJ; 1989).
5. Bullough, V. & Bullough, B., *Sin, Sickness & Sanity* (Meridian Books, NY; 1977).
6. Plummer, Kenneth, *The Making of the Modern Homosexual* (Barnes & Noble, Totowa, NY; 1981).
7. Mains, *Urban Aboriginals*, 52.
8. Brame/Jacobs, *Different Loving*, 29.

9. Townsend, *Leathermen's Handbook II*, 20.
10. Mains, *Urban Aboriginals*, 180.

CHAPTER 3: THE SM INDIVIDUAL

1. Brame/Jacobs, *Different Loving*, 43.
2. Henkin, William, writing in *Different Loving*.
3. *Id.*
4. Townsend, *Leathermen's Handbook II*, 19.
5. Moser, Dr. Charles, *An Exploration-Descriptive Study of a Self-Defined S/M (Sado-masochism) Sample, Unpublished doctorial dissertation*, Institute for Advanced Study of Human Sexuality, San Francisco, 1979.
6. Spengler, Andreas, *Manifest Sadomasochism of Males: Results of an Empirical Study*, Archives of Sexual Behavior, 1977.

CHAPTER 4: GETTING THERE: DOWN THE YELLOW BRICK ROAD

1. Lipschutz, Barbara, Cathexis: A Preliminary Investigation into the Nature of SM, *What Color is Your Handkerchief?: A Lesbian SM Sexuality Reader*, [eds. Samous], (Berkeley, CA.; Samois).
2. Mains, *Urban Aboriginals*, 153.
3. Samois, *Coming to Power*, 219.
4. Mains, *Urban Aboriginals*, 24.
5. Samois, *Coming to Power*, 223.
6. Mains, *Urban Aboriginals*, 26.
7. Samois, *Coming to Power*, 223.
8. *Id.* at 61.
9. Mains, *Urban Aboriginals, 173.*

CHAPTER 5: BUILDING BLOCKS: TRUST AND CONSENT

1. Miller/Devon, *Screw the Roses, Send Me the Thorns*, 56.
2. Samois, *Coming to Power*, 107.
3. Brame/Jacobs, *Different Loving*, 52.

CHAPTER 6: WHY ON EARTH DO WE DO THIS STUFF?

1. Samois, *Coming to Power*, 193.
2. Rosen, Michael, *Sexual Magic: The SM Photographs*, (Shaynew Press, San Francisco, 1986).
3. Gini Graham Scott, *Erotic Power*, 37.
4. *Id.*
5. Samous, *Coming to Power*, 37.
6. Brame/Jacobs, *Differing Loving*, 67.

CHAPTER 7: ROLES: TO HAVE OR BE HAD: THAT IS THE QUESTION

1. Miller/Devon, *Screw the Roses, Send Me the Thorns*, 19.
2. Mains, *Urban Aboriginals*, 83.
3. Brame/Jacobs, *Different Loving*, 17.
4. Miller/Devon, *Screw the Roses, Send Me the Thorns*, 41.
5. Brame/Jacobs, *Different Loving*, 56.
6. Miller/Devon, *Screw the Roses, Send Me the Thorns*, 190.

7. Samois, *Coming to Power*, 36.
8. *Id.* at 35.
9. Miller/Devon, *Screw the Roses, Send Me the Thorns*, 17.
10. Samois, *Coming to Power*, 95.
11. "Ask the Columnist," reprinted by permission of R. L. Smith, Society of Janus newsletter, Growing Pains.
12. Samois, *Coming to Power*, 59.
13. *Id.* at 107.
14. *Id.* at 190.
15. Rand, Ayn, *Atlas Shrugged.*
16. Miller/Devon, *Screw the Roses, Send Me the Thorns*, 56.
17. *Id.* at 62.
18. *Id.* at 192.
19. Samois, *Coming to Power*, 190.
20. Reik, Theodor, *Masochism & Modern Man.*
21. Mains, *Urban Aboriginals*, 137.
22. "Ask the Columnist," reprinted by permission of R. L. Smith, Society of Janus newsletter, *Growing Pains.*
23. Mains, *Urban Aboriginals*, 74.
24. Miller/Devon, *Screw the Roses, Send Me the Thorns*, 9.
25. Samois, *Coming to Power*, 51.

CHAPTER 8: THE NUTS AND BOLTS OF WHIPS AND CHAINS

1. William Henkin, Ph.D., writing in *Different Loving*, 37.
2. *DungeonMaster* magazines, San Francisco, California.
3. Miller/Devon, *Screw the Roses, Send Me the Thorns*, 64.
4. Brame/Jacobs, *Different Loving*, 51.
5. Mains, *Urban Aboriginals*, 54.
6. "Ask the Columnist," reprinted by permission of R. L. Smith, Society of Janus newsletter, *Growing Pains*, 12/95.
7. "Ask the Columnist," reprinted by permission of R. L. Smith, Society of Janus newsletter, *Growing Pains.*
8. Mains, *Urban Aboriginals*. 88.
9. Miller/Devon, *Screw the Roses, Send Me the Thorns*, 94.
10. Sprinkel, Stephen, Gannett News Service, *Oakland Tribune* (4/5/82).
11. Samois, *Coming to Power*, 70.

CHAPTER 9: PAIN: AN EXQUISITE AGONY

1. Mains, *Urban Aboriginals*, 61.
2. *Id.* at 62.
3. *Id.* at 50.
4. *Id.* at 58.
5. *Id.* at 154.
6. *Id.* at 103.
7. Interview with filmmaker Wakefield Poole, *Drummer* magazine 27, 1978, p. 14.
8. Brame/Jacobs, *Different Loving*, 43.
9. Novel, citation unknown.
10. Mains, *Urban Aboriginals*, 59.
11. *Id.* at 59.
12. Samois, *Coming to Power*, 35.
13. Mains, *Urban Aboriginals*, 61.

14. Brame/Jacobs, *Different Loving*, 67.
15. Mains, *Urban Aboriginals*, 69.
16. *Id.* at 137.
17. Samois, *Coming to Power*, 185.
18. Mains, *Urban Aboriginals*, 50.
19. Rand, Ayn, *Atlas Shrugged*.

CHAPTER 10: MEETING OTHERS

1. Ian Young, Karla Jay & Allen Young, eds. *Lavender Culture* (Jove/HBS Books, 1979) 85–117.
2. Mains, *Urban Aboriginals*, 30.
3. *Id.* at 28.
4. Young, Ian, *Lavender Culture*.
5. Lee, John, *The Social Organization of Sexual Risk*, Alternative Lifestyles (1979).
6. Wiseman, Jay, *SM 101* (San Francisco, 1993).
7. Mains, *Urban Aboriginals*, 141.
8. "Ask the Columnist," reprinted by permission of R. L. Smith, Society of Janus newsletter, *Growing Pains*. 12/95.

CHAPTER 11: SM, POLITICS, AND THE LAW

1. Dear Abby, Syndicated newspaper column, 6/6/87.
2. Samois, *Coming to Power*, 200.
3. *Id.* at 61.
4. *Against Sadomasochism*, eds. Linden/Pagano et al. (San Francisco: Frog in the Well, 1982).
5. *Id.*
6. Samois, *Coming to Power*, 86.
7. *Id.* at 85.
8. *Id.*
9. Linden/Pagano, eds., *Against Sadomasochism*, 19 and 30.
10. Samois, *Coming to Power*, 223.
11. *Id.* at 215.
12. *Id.* at 183.
13. Mains, *Urban Aboriginals*, 155.
14. Townsend, *Leathermen's Handbook II*, 24.
15. Samois, *Coming to Power*, 31.

CHAPTER 12: THE DOWNSIDE OF THE DARKSIDE

1. Samois, *Coming to Power*, 204.

ODDS AND ENDS

1. "Ask the Columnist," reprinted by permission of R. L. Smith, Society of Janus newsletter, *Growing Pains*. 8/95.

Acknowledgments

Special thanks to Bruce G., Pat B., Byron, Phil and August, Marsha, Tiffany, Joe and Kate, Bill and Jules, Grant Morgan, and Jackie Davison for all their help, and to all those in the SM community who chipped in with support, patience, and love.

▼ ▼ ▼

Every reasonable effort has been made to locate the owners of rights to previously published material reprinted in this book. The authors and publisher gratefully acknowledge the following:

Thanks to Mark Thompson, Geoff Mains's *Urban Aboriginals* (Gay Sunshine Press); Philip Miller and Molly Devon, *Screw the Roses, Send Me the Thorns* (Mystic Rose Press).

Taken from the DEAR ABBY column by Abigail Van Buren © 1987 UNIVERSAL PRESS SYNDICATE. Reprinted with permission. All rights reserved.

Of related interest from Continuum

Rob Baker

The Art of AIDS: From Stigma to Conscience

The first comprehensive exploration of the aesthetic dimensions of the AIDS epidemic. "Rob Baker was one of the first—and one of the very best—to write seriously about pop culture in the sixties. Now he gives us an essential, remarkably concise, analytic yet personal, and constantly readable overview of plague art."—LINDA WINER, *New York Newsday*

252 pages 0-8264-0653-X $24.95

Robert T. Francouer, Editor-in-Chief; Martha Cornog, Timothy Perper, and Norman A. Scherzer, Coeditors

The Complete Dictionary of Sexology

New Expanded Edition

Now in paperback. With detailed definitions of more than six thousand sexually related terms, this is the most comprehensive dictionary of sexuality in the English language.

"Well executed . . . a remarkable job."—*Booklist*

800 pages 0-8264-0672-6 $29.95 paperback

Sigmund Freud

Psychological Writings and Letters

Edited by Sander L. Gilman

The classic works on sexuality, infant sexuality, dreams, psychological procedure, telepathy, jokes, and the uncanny—also featuring a selection of Freud's correspondence.

324 pages 0-8264-0723-4 $14.95 paperback; 0-8264-0722-6 $29.50 hardcover

Donald McCormick

Erotic Literature: A Connoisseur's Guide

"Truly a connoisseur's guide, *Erotic Literature* serves as both a reminder of the centrality of sexuality to human experience and a guide to its artistic celebration in world literature."—*Wilson Library Bulletin*

288 pages 0-8264-0594-0 $14.95 paperback

John Money

Reinterpreting the Unspeakable: Human Sexuality 2000

A ground-breaking and essential manual for the complete interviewer in clinical practice. "Dr. John Money was one of my principal influences when I was writing *Sexual Personae*. He is the leading sexologist in the world today."—CAMILLE PAGLIA

252 pages 0-8264-0651-3 $29.95

Dr. Ruth Westheimer

Dr. Ruth's Encyclopedia of Sex

An authoritative work on all facets of sexuality, for home or school library, edited by the internationally famous sex educator.

"Entries address all aspects of sexuality—from mechanics and biology, to cultural, legal, and religious concerns. The range of material covered in this volume is impressive."—*Publishers Weekly*

312 pages 7" x 10" 0-8264-0625-4 $29.50

Available at your bookstore or from the publisher: **The Continuum Publishing Company, 370 Lexington Avenue, New York, NY 10017 1-800-937-5557**